Unbreakable

Unbreakable

**HOW TO THRIVE UNDER
FEAR-BASED LEADERS**

Kate Lowry

Copyright © 2025 by Kate Lowry

All rights reserved.

No part of this book may be reproduced, or stored in a retrieval system, or transmitted in any form or by any means, electronic, mechanical, photocopying, recording, or otherwise, without express written permission of the publisher.

Without in any way limiting the author's and publisher's exclusive rights under copyright, any use of this publication to "train" generative artificial intelligence (AI) technologies to generate text is expressly prohibited. The author reserves all rights to license uses of this work for generative AI training and development of machine learning language models.

Some names and identifying details have been changed to protect the privacy of individuals.

Published by Scaleheart Press, Los Altos, California
www.scaleheart.co

Edited and designed by Girl Friday Productions
www.girlfridayproductions.com

Cover design: Greg Mortimer

Image credits: cover © iStock/hocus-focus

Disclaimer: This book shares information intended to help you navigate difficult circumstances from fear-based leadership tactics. However, the information in this book is not intended to provide or be a substitute for professional medical or legal advice. Please seek out professional medical care or legal advice as appropriate if you are feeling unsafe, experiencing mental health challenges, or navigating possible legal consequences from interactions with individuals engaging in fear-based leadership tactics or manipulative behaviors, or if you are concerned about physical, mental, or emotional harm in any way. Always seek out the care and attention you need to be well.

Certain concepts discussed in this book are based on long-standing principles of social science research, management science, and professional coaching. References to specific resources are referenced in footnotes and endnotes. Readers are encouraged to explore these and other resources.

ISBN (paperback): 979-8-218-76706-8
ISBN (ebook): 979-8-218-76707-5

First edition

To all who hold the light on the path for others.

To all who need someone to believe in them.

To all who feel alone in the face of a bully.

This book is for you.

Contents

Preface xi

Before We Begin: Resilient Roots Make Room for Strategy

Identity Diversification for Resilience: Adding Legs
    to Your Stool 3
Who We Love (Source of Identity #1) 5
Our Values (Source of Identity #2) 10
Our Abilities (Source of Identity #3) 12
Our Physical Selves (Source of Identity #4) 14
Our Social Background (Source of Identity #5) 18
Where We Come From (Source of Identity #6) 20

Part One: Identifying and Understanding Fear-Based Leaders

An Insult to Their Intelligence: Understanding
    the Mind of a Fear-Based Leader 25
Insecurity Drives the Train: They're Deeply Insecure 31
It's a Real Shame: Shame Fuels Them 36
Secret Tests: They're Grading You 42
Clocking and Tailoring to Emotional Maturity Levels:
    They're Not Really Adults 46
Outdated Models: They're Out of Date 52
The Vulnerabilities of the Arrogant: They Have Big Blind Spots . . 55
Playing Realities: They're Not in Reality 58

Forgive and Forget Is for Fools: They Have Long Memories . . . 63
It Will Never Be Me: Tactics Work Predictably on Them 66
Key Takeaways and Reflection Questions 69

*Part Two: The Tool Kit: Specific Strategies for How to
Thrive Under Fear-Based Authoritarian Leaders*

Send in the Clowns, They're Already Here:
    How to Upwardly Manage Fear-Based Leaders 73
Sweat Them with Silence: Availability Is Leverage 77
Painting in Gray in a Black-and-White World:
    Embrace Nuance 80
Starve the Dragon: Put Them on an Attention Diet 83
Move Fast and Break Things: Destruction Is the Point 86
I Own You: You Are a Possession 89
When They Make You See Red: How to Anchor 93
Negotiating with Thieves: How to Rig the Game 96
Don't Shop for Milk at the Hardware Store:
    Know What They're Good For 99
A Lesson in Discernment: Actions vs. Words 103
You're Just Imagining Things: How to Resist Brainwashing . . . 108
Control Over Connection: How to Bend, Not Snap 111
Fewer and Better: How to Prioritize 114
Familiarity ≠ Safety: Don't Get Comfortable 117
No One Can Cage You Without Your Consent: Find the Space . . 121
You Have Permission to Move: Get Unstuck 124
False Generosity: Find the String 127
Finding Good Pockets in Bad Places: Learn to Diligence 130
Power Corrupts: How to Stay Whole 133

The Sword of Perception: How to See Through Halos 136
Misleading Marketing: How Not to Fall for It 142
If You Give a Mouse a Cookie: How to Avoid Slippery Slopes . . 145
Manufactured Chaos: It's Intentional 148
Learn Their Buttons, Then Press the Keys: Set Strategic Traps . . 151
Key Takeaways and Reflection Questions 155

Part Three: Navigating Systems and Safety

Recognizing Stalking, Safety Risks, and Control Tactics 161
Archetypes of Half-Safe Controllers 169
Guide to Physical Safety 173
Guide to Cyber Security 177
If You're Asked to Do Something Illegal 180
How to Find, Select, Pitch, and Retain Lawyers 182
When Part of Your Tool Kit Gets Taken Away 194
When You Lose It All and Have to Start Over 198
Deciding Who to Trust 201
When Relationships Don't Fit Right Anymore 205
Safeguarding Your Energy 208
The Cost of Seeing 211
Parting Words: I Am Water 213

Acknowledgments 216
About the Author 219

Preface

Fear-based leaders have been around since the dawn of the human race. There have always been, and always will be, people who abuse positions of power to dominate, control, and subjugate others, simply because they can. They are in every part of the world—every culture, every type of organization, from kindergarten classes to boardrooms—if you haven't met one yet, you will someday.

However, in the last five years, something has changed. It used to be that motivating through top-down, scare-tactic, threat-based leadership was a no-no. Something that people knew was wrong, and at least tried to disguise as something else. But recently, this type of behavior has become not only permissible, but openly celebrated by many—and when there is more permission to behave this way, the gloves come off.

I have had over twenty-five managers in my career, and when I started out, 30 percent of the leaders I encountered in the elite business world were like this. In the last few years, 80 percent were.

This means that there is an incredible need for a tactical guide of how to upwardly manage this type of person—how to not only survive, but thrive—so that you can protect what you care about and live the life you want to live, despite the storm cloud hanging over you.

This book is designed to be that guide—to explain how these types of people think, act, and make decisions, so that you can anticipate and respond to their behavior in ways that preserve autonomy, agency, and empowerment.

These types of leaders deeply affect the people around them, and engender a sense of powerlessness—so if there is one thing that you take away from this book, it is that you are not powerless, but incredibly powerful. I know because I have been surrounded by people like this since my first days on earth, and have been able to take back control and live a wonderful life. This book will show you how to do that.

It is all grounded in real-world examples from my life as someone who has spent thirty-plus years testing every type of strategy against these fear-based folks, organized into a system of tools to help you operate in a culture of fear, upwardly manage difficult people, and stay safe in the process.

If you read all of this and it sounds like this couldn't be real, that's a good thing. To people who haven't experienced these types of cruel, vindictive people, my writing might sound hyperbolic. I can assure you that it is not; these are all real examples. I have chosen those that are the most benign and least harsh so that it's not excessively shocking, but be aware that these are not exaggerations. Some fear-based leaders are more subtle, and some are more obvious, but their motives and tactics, whether hidden or overt, tend to be the same.

The book is structured first to teach you how to shore up resilience, because if your tank is empty, then you cannot effectively use tactics that take energy and wherewithal to execute. It then teaches you how to predict, understand, and manage this type of leader, before moving into more specific guidance around security, legal action, and stakeholder management.

If you're starting out feeling alone, hopeless, or afraid—know that I am with you, and that there is a light at the end of this tunnel. You will need to think flexibly, act strategically, and invest in learning—but you are going to make it to the other side.

Before We Begin

*Resilient Roots Make
Room for Strategy*

Identity Diversification for Resilience: Adding Legs to Your Stool

A lot of people seem to be getting sandbagged by life right now. They are overwhelmed, confused, frozen, and worn down. So, how do you shore up your resilience in a world that can be hard to tolerate?

The key is in diversifying your sources of identity. The more sources of identity you have, the stronger a leader you are. It's a lot like sitting on a stool. Let me show you what I mean.

If Jeff works eighty hours a week for his company, doesn't have hobbies, and doesn't have relationships, because the main, number one thing he is is a CTO at Widget Co., then his list of identities looks like:

- CTO at Widget Co.

His stool has one single leg holding it up. This means that if Jeff gets laid off from Widget Co., and someone kicks that leg under, his *entire foundation of who he is crumbles*. He is totally unmoored, and has nothing to lean back on.

But if we look at his colleague Amara, the head of RevOps at Widget Co., it's a different story. She's in an '80s punk band, is an aunt to her nieces and nephews, crochets scarves while watching *Days of Our Lives*, and owns a dog. It might *sound* at first glance that Jeff is more successful. But if we look at her identities list, it comes out to:

- Head of RevOps at Widget Co.
- Aunt to Jami and Jessie
- Lead singer of Sound Trash
- Crocheter
- *Days of Our Lives* fan
- Sparky's number one owner

If *she* gets laid off in the same hostile takeover as Jeff, and someone kicks her stool's work leg out from under her, *five other legs are holding her up*.

This type of thinking is critical to understanding how to survive in environments of uncertainty.

A lot of identities are feeling isolated right now. My hope is that sharing different sources of my identity will help you feel less alone.

Who We Love
(Source of Identity #1)

One of the most powerful sources of identity is who we love. Maybe you're a parent, a child, a partner—it all means something. Here is a piece I wrote several years ago, about how I love:

I have always been someone who doesn't talk about who and how I love, because I've never thought I should have to. Straight people never have to announce their most private thoughts or desires. Unless I've heard someone in my life tell me directly, I assume that I do not know their predilections (rather than mentally assigning a default that has to be changed, let people write their own stories). I have also never wanted my sexuality to be the first thing people think of when they think of me. It's just one attribute of my being, like being blue eyed or tall or slightly clumsy. I'd rather let thoughtful, creative, or other adjectives come to mind, and for many people, once they label someone as different, sexuality is the first thing they then think of. They become "Jeff, who you know is gay" or some variation of that.

Professionally, I used to never want people to think about any of my physical attributes, at all. If I could have existed as an androgynous, featureless blob in every work meeting so no one would ever judge me by my gender or appearance, I would have. This is because I have heard of investors in the Valley who won't fund fat people, had male bosses lecture me that I'm not impressed enough by them, and seen endless cases of colleagues being passed over for promotions or assignments due to gender. Work to me is for building things together and exchanging ideas, and it's not someplace I felt comfortable being completely authentic because I saw every day how minority groups are treated differently. I know that good workplaces see and honor diversity as a strength, but I have faced a lot of discrimination in past positions that suggested to me we are not there yet as a society. It was hard for me to believe that any workplace was truly "safe" to be out, to disclose disabilities, and so on, because workplaces are made of people, and people in this century are still often very entrenched in bias.

While I know now that no place is free of bias, my thinking has shifted because the cost is too high for me to not be myself at work each day. But there are still plenty of challenging attitudes that I encounter regularly. Many people don't respect boundaries, make unfair assumptions, or feel like their curiosity is more important than my comfort. Here is how I answer their questions:

No, how I identify doesn't mean I was any less committed in past relationships. No, it doesn't mean I'm a promiscuous person. No, I didn't "turn gay" from going to a women's college. No, it's not a phase; in hindsight, the earliest memories I have about it relate to being ten years old. No, it doesn't mean I have twice the playing field, and I am not "lucky" because of that.

No, it's not a moot point in my life if you see me choose to date men. No, I'm not less LGBTQ+ because I'm not "fully gay" or can pass as straight. No, I don't have a crush on you just because you're female and my friend. Oh, you always knew something was different about me? Great, yes, I am an accomplished musician, management consultant, product strategist, startup founder, writer, photographer, and cook. No, I will not go kiss a girl to prove it to you. No, a bad experience did not "scare me off men." No, I do not have an obligation to go explore all the options out there in lieu of loving and stable long-term relationships.

No, I will not tell you about my relationship history because it's suddenly interesting to you. No, it's not something I chose to make myself feel special—at the time I realized it myself years ago, I was young, completely confused, very Catholic, and unhappy and in denial of this aspect of myself. It felt monumentally inconvenient and unwelcome and it took a year to adjust and accept it as a possible part of my identity, because I had been taught people who are different were something to be afraid of. It had never occurred to me that being anything but straight was even an option in my world, and it was a complete surprise to me.

Most people are attracted to some people, and for me that group happens to be gender agnostic. A person is a person in my book of attraction, and the author is not available for comment. And that's cool and should be fine, but it initially caused a lot of fear for me. It feels like wondering if every person you meet will randomly potentially hate you for having blond hair or a certain favorite ice cream flavor. I grew up hearing whispers about "he-shes" and scandalous people who "batted for both teams." At college, people talked about LUGs, lesbians until graduation. I've had past coworkers tell me directly that gay people should have to use separate stores or not be able to go to the same banks—that it would be a boon to the economy. When I reported that and other behaviors, I was told to keep my head down and that I should be glad I hadn't heard worse. It took me almost two years to join my employer's LGBTQ+ affinity group as a full member because at the time, I was the only out pan or bi member in the entire Midwest office, and was very invisible having a male significant other. Even the GLAM leadership were confused what to do with me.

But, it helped me provide more exposure and visibility to others, and that was important to me. I served as a Facebook recruiting ambassador and have held other similar positions at work because often it feels like bi and pan people are an afterthought in queer communities. Characters in TV shows, like Kalinda, Blake, and Kat on *The Good Wife* and *Madam Secretary*, and figures like Miley Cyrus, Cara Delevingne, Demi Lovato, and Antoni Porowski have helped assert these identities, but there are still a lot of assumptions that depending on who you are dating, you are lurching between or testing out the gay or straight camps like some sort of fun game. To that I say, it doesn't feel like that. It feels like being a person who, like most other people, loves some other person. In love you exist in time alone, the two of you with secret looks and inside jokes, and only when you step out into the sun holding hands does the world react differently for some reason based on the type of hand you're holding.

When I first came out years ago, I wondered if my voice would be less believed on other issues because I could be more broadly discounted as part of another minority group. You may not realize it, but I and anyone else in the LGBTQ+ community could still be arrested in seventy countries. But, people don't have to like me, just not treat me like I'm a second-class citizen—just for being who I am.

For many others like me who come from conservative, religious, or homophobic families, it's okay to not be ready to be fully public about it. The important thing is that you know you are wonderful the way you are, no matter how you love.

Our Values
(Source of Identity #2)

Another core source of identity is your values. When I make choices in my life, I make them based on what will most honor my core values—things like integrity, curiosity, and compassion—in combination with what is strategic. In companies, knowing the firm's values in priority order is what allows employees to make decisions in the absence of leadership. Personally, if you don't know what you stand for, you may never stand up. So, what do you value?

Independence and healthy interdependence
Respect and safety
Allyship Equality
Humor and joy Advocacy
Curiosity Personal responsibility
Warmth
Integrity
Open-mindedness Stability
Kindness and gentleness
Clear and honest communication
Connection and reciprocity
Authenticity Gratitude
Showing up Learning and self-development
Wellness and self care
Trying Self-trust

Our Abilities (Source of Identity #3)

Another critical source is our abilities. I have a lot of those, but what I'm *more* interested in talking about are my disabilities—because my disabilities are part of what makes me strong.

Over the last two years, I have had over eight hundred doctor appointments. I take lifesaving medications nine times a day in order to function, all timed at specific intervals. I have to complete therapies each week, or I could end up back in the hospital. On the surface, that might *sound* like a liability—until you look closer.

I get more done in three hours than most of my colleagues do in an entire day—because I don't have the *option* to work slower. I am adaptable to the extreme, because in the morning I could be fine, and ten hours later I might be in the ER. *Nothing throws me.*

I am *creative*, because I have to track my health symptoms hour by hour, every day, and decide on the fly what tools in my arsenal are most appropriate for each symptom flare—meds, IVs, rest, therapies. My *triage muscle* is as good as an ER nurse's, because in the last ten years, I have had high-stakes decision-making reps times a thousand—because every day, one path I choose could leave me too dizzy to walk, and the other could mean I get to sleep that night instead of lying awake with a tachy heart.

My *strategy muscle* is more like a sixty-year-old CEO's, because my *daily stakeholder set* includes thirty executives at work and in my coaching and advising practice, multiple legal and security professionals, and twenty high-ego medical professionals, all of whom think their issue or approach is the most important. I have to manage, direct, and cajole them to keep the whole group functioning and moving in the same direction, while making serious decisions about how to phase treatments that affect my wellbeing and that of others. The information sharing, prioritization, and team management is an *art form*.

When you think of the areas of your life that may be discounted by colleagues—having kids, having disabilities, needing to care for family—what strengths do those parts of your life truly bring?

Our Physical Selves (Source of Identity #4)[1]

In ways that can be hard to admit, our physical selves are part of the way we move through the world. In my case, my path is sometimes easier because I am tall, or because I am pale; and it's sometimes harder, because I look young, because I am blond, and because I am overweight. In particular, fatness is not something that gets talked

---

1. This piece draws from:
    - Eidelson, Josh. "Yes, You Can Still Be Fired for Being Fat." Businessweek, March 15, 2022. https://www.bloomberg.com/news/features/2022-03-15/weight-discrimination-remains-legal-in-most-of-the-u-s.
    - Fulton, Melody, Sriharsha Dadana, and Vijay N. Srinivasan. "Obesity, Stigma, and Discrimination." StatPearls. October 26, 2023. https://www.ncbi.nlm.nih.gov/books/NBK554571/.
    - SHRM. "New SHRM Research Details Weight Discrimination in the Workplace." May 8, 2023. https://www.shrm.org/about/press-room/new-shrm-research-details-weight-discrimination-in-the-workplace.

about enough in Silicon Valley, so that's why I'm writing about it here. By and large, there are not a lot of fat knowledge workers in the Bay. For example, I only met two in my entire time at Meta, out of hundreds of colleagues.

To be clear—I love every inch of my body. It has worked harder for me than I will ever know. Whatever size I am, I am proud of it. I have been a size 4 (S), and also a size 18 (XL). In the last couple of years, during treatment for intense illness, I had to make a choice: take meds that would let me have a dramatically improved quality of life, with a potential side effect of gaining weight, or potentially be disabled to the point of not being able to work. I chose the meds along with other treatments, and my quality of life improved in amazing ways. As a side effect, I gained ninety pounds in three years.

I was so scared! To have my body change that much so fast was alarming. I have stretch marks, and have had to rebuy clothes over and over. But I was most afraid of how the world would see me differently. I have always been health conscious—I eat a plant-based diet, go to therapy, have a dietitian and a trainer, and work out four times a week. But a few years ago, as this started happening, I began to feel self-conscious at the gym. At restaurants, I would see my reflection in the window, and feel shame for my size, wondering if people would judge me if I had dessert or something less "healthy" by non-intuitive-eating standards.

I was scared because I had heard stories. For instance, one of my friends, when fundraising for their startup, was told by a top venture capitalist (VC) that they'd only do the round if the fat founder was kicked off the cap table. Plus, I knew the stats:

- Overweight people are hired less, promoted less, and paid less. For every six pounds an American woman gains, she is paid 2% less.
- Studies show that fat people are often *seen* as lazy, lacking self-control, and irresponsible.
- Primary care doctors spend less time with fat patients because they view them as noncompliant.

That isn't okay. And I wanted to do my part to change the status quo, because all bodies are good bodies. So here are some other important facts (all vetted by my dietitian):

- People can be healthy at almost any size.
- Obesity is a very complicated disease that cannot be distilled to calories in, calories out—in fact, sometimes reducing caloric intake leads to gaining weight, because your metabolism slows down.
- Restrictive diets are clinically proven not to work—and the weight cycling they cause can be very dangerous to people's health.
- Calorie restriction more often than not leads to binge eating.

- Sugar intake has no proven causal relationship to insulin resistance.
- There are many things that can lead to being fat, and rarely is it related to self-control. People can be fat due to genetics, medications, trauma coping mechanisms, eating disorders, poverty-created food deserts, and for so many more reasons.
- It is never okay to comment on people's weight loss, or weight gain. Some people who are very ill get lots of compliments on their weight loss when they want nothing more than to keep it on, and it's distressing to hear people congratulate them. Also, some people gain weight on purpose, and others, because they can't help it.

As time went on, I started to realize that the people who mattered didn't care, and the people who cared, didn't matter. I will always be glad when someone who judges me for my weight chooses to steer clear of me, or underestimate me. Because I love myself—and my body too.

Our Social Background (Source of Identity #5)

Many people do not like to think about their class of origin, because it can make people feel less self-made—or, because they want to leave the hungry days behind them.

I grew up with a foot in both worlds. Growing up, living with my mother after my parents' divorce, we mostly had *enough*, but we had to move a lot, because rent was too expensive. One year, we lived in a three-room cabin in the woods, heated by a woodstove, where my mom slept on the pullout couch so that I could have a bedroom. We would make snow cones out of the actual snow outside, and pick mulberries on the side of the road.

But, my middle-class parents got me into a school district meant for wealthy children, because the school didn't have enough children in their exempted village to fill it up. And so I learned a lot of things. For one, that the kids with ten pairs of Ugg boots were still often miserable, with stepparents on drugs and their boyfriends assaulting them, while others used their wealth to create a sense of calm and safety in their worlds. I also learned how to talk, and think, like the elite. I worked hard and earned a ticket into the world of private liberal arts colleges, management consulting, and later on, venture capital and private equity.

When I began working in consulting, I was shocked that my $135 meal per diem was more than my family spent on groceries in a week. And each time I "leveled up" in my career, for a long time, there was still a part of me inside whose eyes would go wide when I heard the scale at which my partners, acquisition targets, and peers thought. Even as I learned how they saw the world, I kept the learnings from my school days in my heart, that *I am their equal* and that *money and power are not, alone, remotely impressive.*

I am not drawn to power, and I am not drawn to money, except to have enough to keep myself healthy, safe, and well. But I tend to think the people who *are* drawn to power are the least deserving to have it, and that the people who *do* have money seldom use it in the ways it could be applied for the biggest impact.

How has your social background impacted the way you see the world?

Where We Come From (Source of Identity #6)

The last source of identity I'd like to discuss is where we come from.

I grew up in a world where manipulation, coercion, and power games were second nature to the authority figures around me. I was steeped and brewed in sexism, racism, homophobia, abuse, neglect, violence, coldness, volatility, and cruelty. It could have destroyed me. Instead, I chose to turn towards the light, do the work, and lean into compassion, and now I am turning it into a blueprint for helping others navigate destructive instability without losing themselves.

Understanding power doesn't mean wielding it unfairly. If anything, survivors of coercion are the ones most committed to resisting it.

I don't believe in power through fear. I believe in

influence through integrity. I don't believe in control. I believe in agency.

Most people who lead with fear are deeply insecure, thin skinned, and brittle. The followership they inspire is not the lasting fealty that they desire, but weak ties of convenience and transaction. And they are so, so predictable.

I believe the world needs values-driven, intentional leaders with both smarts and hearts, and I plan to teach all of the ways that I learned to survive and thrive in environments ruled by fear and destruction to help make that more probable.

I hope that, in this book, you enjoy the homespun lessons mixed in with those from my experiences in the high-stakes worlds of startups, VC, big tech, and management consulting, and the safe spaces I create in my executive coaching and advising practice.

Part One

*Identifying and Understanding
Fear-Based Leaders*

An Insult to Their Intelligence: Understanding the Mind of a Fear-Based Leader

Right now, fear-based leaders are having a moment. By that, I mean leaders who posture dominance, and then threaten their direct reports with impunity, expecting the direct reports to *jump*. And, because of this, a lot of people need to adapt very quickly.

Luckily, you have me, and this guide to top-down leadership 101. I know these blustery asshole types, and I'm going to teach you how they think, and why they act the way they do, so you can decide how you want to take them on. Without understanding their mental blueprint, their actions will feel capricious and random, not predictable—but I promise, once you can tilt into their worldview, you'll be able to navigate it well yourself.

First, let's go inside the mind of a fear-based leader (yuck!).

The most important thing to understand is the concept of the *pedestal*. Imagine the leader on a throne on a pedestal, with everyone else beneath them. You might think, "Can't I just climb up to meet them?" *No.* In their world, in their mind, *no one is their equal, ever.* There are only people *above* and *below*. There is *no such thing as equality, and connection is for the weak.* This means that to them, they are either stepping on others, or being stepped on.

The next piece you need to understand is *win/loss* thinking. Why is this important? Life isn't a game, right? *To them, it is.* And if you're not *winning*, then you're *losing*. Every single thing they do is to be more of a *winner* and to avoid being a *loser*.

But if they were just hypercompetitive, that would be one thing. The real problem is they aren't just trying to win—they have no clue who they really are.

I need you to imagine that you have no self-awareness, just a sloppily constructed scarecrow in your mind of what you look like to the outside world. This means that with no self-awareness, there is *no such thing as a double standard*—and even better if the double standard is projection (saying something to others that is actually about yourself). When the subconscious doesn't get noticed by the conscious mind, it starts manifesting to the people around you.

If you hear a fear-based leader insulting the people around them, immediately replace "you" with "I," and you will have a direct channel to their inner monologue.

> **Example:** "You idiot betas have no clue what you're doing. Even your own mothers probably don't love you. Don't come back to me until you've done better."

> **What this really means:** "I have no idea what I'm doing. Even my own mother didn't love me. I'm not good enough."

Next, I need you to understand the concept of *constraints* that fear-based leaders act within. The key mistake to avoid is thinking within *frameworks or rules*. These guys are very predictable, but not if you think in a system of rules. If you do that, you will fail to anticipate future actions. To understand their next move, stop asking yourself, "Is this allowed?" Instead, ask, "What's the boldest power play you could pull off if you thought risk and rules did not exist for you?"

To these leaders, *rules* and *limits* are an *insult* to their intelligence, meant for *lesser peons*, not *kings*.

You need to expect *end runs around the limits*—if you're thinking in rules, you might ask, "Why would this

CEO risk alienating his board?" In actuality, his endgame is to become chairman, expand the board by four seats, and remove all the other members. Or, maybe he's planning on selling his shares in the company, quitting, joining a competitor as CEO, then acquiring the company back for him to run with no oversight.

Because, to someone who sees *rules and limits* as an *insult, accountability and oversight* are *anathema*. It feels to them like a parent giving a seventeen-year-old a babysitter. No thanks, Mom! GTFO and let me have my party.

So if they're not about facts or rules, what are they about?

They play in a field of *emotion, dominance,* and *control.*

This means that if you're speaking rules and they're speaking emotions, you're *on different radio channels.* They hear you as static and you hear them in a land of logic, and that is *the wrong way to translate what they're saying.*

That means that you have to be able to speak to the *gist* of what they're saying if you want to go toe to toe with them.

Incendiary statements have a *surface meaning* and then a *real gist.* In a *logical reply* the surface meaning equals the gist. A reply corrected to their emotional radio channel responds to *the gist,* not the surface meaning.

Example:

> **Fear-based leader says an emotion-based statement:** "I'm going to fire all of you by the end of the week if you don't launch the MVP tomorrow."
>
> **Gist:** "I am in control and I want you to know it."
>
> **C-1 report says a logical reply:** "But, sir, that's impossible, that will take two months at minimum."
>
> **Gist:** "But, sir, that's impossible, that will take two months at minimum."
>
> **Leader hears it as:** "I defy your control."
>
> **C-1 report says a radio-channel-corrected reply:** "Yes sir, right away, sir."
>
> **Gist:** "I respect you and your control."

The first response makes the leader want to smash the direct report for defiance. The second response allows business to move along as usual. Because, it *doesn't matter* that the full MVP is not launched tomorrow. You could launch literally any half-completed version of a product and tell them it was the MVP. What matters is that you *heard their request for confirmation of respect and gave them the correct answer.* Bonus points for you, you now have loyalty in the bank and will get more freedom to run your domain as you see fit!

Insecurity Drives the Train: They're Deeply Insecure

True leaders are motivated by a desire to do right by the world—to leave it better than they found it. In contrast, a *fear-based* leader is someone who is driven primarily by *fear* and *insecurity.*

Two important truths about this type of "leader":

1. Their deep-seated insecurities and fears are what keep them in motion—fear they're not enough, fear they don't know what they're doing, fear they're not loved.
2. Because *they* are driven by their own fears and insecurities, they assume this is the best way to *motivate others*. While this is short-term, wishful thinking that is not *remotely*

backed by any type of management science, this means that instead of leading through *inspiration, example,* and *influence,* they attempt to control by leading through *blustering, posturing, threatening, attacking,* and *defending.*

This does not work. It creates the impression of initial results, which is misleading, but the impacts are not lasting.

Imagine that you're asleep in your room, and someone runs in and screams at you, "Time to get up and run four miles! You have five minutes to get out or I'll chop off your head!"

You will jump out of your bed, probably stumble out the door, and run. But you may also forget your shoes, sprain your ankle on the stairs, and collapse halfway through the jog because you're feeling sick.

Now imagine that your friend calls you the day before, and says, "Hey, I'm so excited to spend time with you tomorrow! Let's run four miles together. I know you're new to running, but we're going to see so many interesting things out there on the trail, and I promise that I'll make sure you can keep pace."

You get up the next day, put on your shoes, and, buoyed by a teammate, make the full run.

Something I want to call out is that in the first scenario, it is *you* vs. *an aggressor.* In the second scenario, it is *you and a friend* against a *challenge.* Fear-based leaders' teams are weak because they set people within their teams, and above and below them, to be in conflict. Strengths-based leaders build *cohesion* in their teams, so that it is not *me vs. you* but *us vs. problem.*

This means that a fear-based leader's team is a lot like ten skinny, brittle strands of thread, tied into a knot and at the end, the leader. Each one of those strands can be snapped with just a little force.

A *strengths-based leader*'s team is like ten strands of thread *spun together* into a small *rope*. When stressors pull on that team from both ends, *cohesion binds them together* and it doesn't snap.

A *fear-based leader* is about *control*. A strengths-based leader is about *activating potential*—unlocking the strengths of each team member, then *getting out of the way* except for the things that *only they can do*. They exist in *service* of their team, not to *extract from it*.

This also impacts *how they motivate*. A fear-based leader uses *extrinsic motivation*—which is momentary. It means using external factors to influence behavior, e.g., "I'll pay you five dollars," or "I'll smack you if you get this wrong."

A strengths-based leader may use a little extrinsic motivation, but primarily focuses on unlocking *intrinsic motivation*—the desire to do something because it is meaningful, interesting, or fulfilling—which is the **single most powerful fuel for sustained performance**. If you can get your team to do things because *they want to* because *they like you, they see how their work contributes to* *the world, and because they enjoy it*—that team will run with you to the ends of the earth. This is where real loyalty, and the safety needed to innovate, comes from.

If intrinsic motivation is a no-brainer, why don't fear-based leaders use it?

1. They can't create the safety needed for this type of excellence. When employees operate under threat, their priority is *self-preservation*, not innovation or quality. This leads to *risk aversion*.
2. Fear leads to *compliance*, not *loyalty*. People might *obey*, but they are afraid to *own their work*. This means if external pressure drops even for a minute, performance crumbles because there was no real *investment* in the outcome—just *avoidance of consequences*. However, all the leader sees is that they obey.
3. Fear suppresses information sharing in order to avoid blame—and if you can't share information to collaborate or show genuine interest without being derided, it's harder to have the freedom for intrinsic motivation. However, all the leader sees is an absence of problems.

Going back to the example of a run, it's pretty clear from an outside perspective that the more constructive approach is more motivating—and ultimately more sustainable. But, in the heart of a fear-based leader, they can't see this because arrogance and insecurity are blinding, and initial compliance makes them *feel* like fear is working. And their blinders mean that they also miss the corresponding *mistakes* that are made, and often hidden.

What do I mean by hidden? Well, in a system where you're *afraid* and held to impossible standards, you can't be anything less than *perfect.* In a single person in a family or a lower-level job, this impacts only a few people—but with leaders, this type of toxicity can be fatal on a massive level.

While I usually write from the perspective of a business leader, the historical example of Mao's famine comes to mind. Mao Zedong's Cultural Revolution was a communist wave of social control in which Chinese society was totally reorganized, and each segment of society was required to produce a certain amount of grain, iron, or other type of resource. The problem was, there was so much intense pressure, instability, and fear used as motivators that there was no *safety* to admit mistakes. So the leaders reporting to Mao lied—they all said their production was great, all quotas were being met. When time came to distribute the harvest, it wasn't there, and millions of people starved to death.

Have you ever felt like you needed to hide something to stay safe? What would it have been like if someone had cared enough to motivate you by making your world engaging, instead?

It's a Real Shame: Shame Fuels Them

Accompanying the fear inside rigid, top-down leaders is shame. Inside each of their heads is an inner critic—a drill sergeant that screams at them, "You're worthless! You don't know what you're doing! My dog could do better than you!"—and this is what keeps them insecure, afraid, and in motion.

Their shame shadows them, tainting their interactions with others—because shame is different than guilt, in that shame says "I am bad," versus guilt, which says "I did something that was bad." Guilt is healthy, in that it can inspire someone to make amends. Shame dominates someone's narrative of who they are, until they are a *reactive* person, not a *responsive* one.

A *reaction* is something reflexive—it's a knee-jerk, first impulse—and a *response* is something *intentional and chosen.* If I get an email about an unexpected obstacle and dash off a fast, angry reply, that is a *reaction*. If I take ten minutes to breathe, think about something else, and come back to it to write a measured, thoughtful reply, then I am *responding.*

Reactive states generally come in four types: fight, flight, freeze, and fawn.[1]

In a *fight state*, which is common with defensive, irascible leaders, they attack all stimulus that they haven't predicted.

In a *flight state*, people try to *escape* stimulus by running away, or mentally disappearing—by being a workaholic, scrolling endlessly, or spacing out.

In a *freeze state*, people are paralyzed into immobility—like a deer that freezes to blend into the forest.

In a *fawn state*, people try to anticipate, predict, and cater to the needs of people around them, before they can be attacked.

Most *fear-based leaders* have a *fight response* reaction type. Their "betas" then flee, freeze, fight, or fawn around them, while the leader exists in a state of perpetual warfare. They are incapable of being responsive, because their window of tolerance for external stimuli is extremely narrow. This means that they have strategy deficits—because strategy requires planning, careful consideration of factors, and the ability to see from other perspectives.

---

1. As defined by Pete Walker.

Here's how this can play out in practice:

- **Fear-based leader:** "This PowerPoint is completely unusable. I don't know how you call yourself analysts. Someone start explaining why this is drivel, now."
- **Freeze response beta:** Stares blankly at the leader, further enraging them.
- **Flight response beta:** Doom scrolls on their phone under the table, looking into their lap.
- **Fawn response beta:** "I'm so sorry, you're right—we should have known this wasn't good enough. Why don't you go home and we'll create a new version right away. In the future, we'll run it past your chief of staff to make sure it's more in line with your standards."

This reactivity leads to a lot of movement based not on strategy, but on *posturing*—similar to how generals in battle may feint their troops into different lines of attack. When these types of leaders meet each other, they are puffing out their chests, and beating on them with their fists, wanting to see who will bow out first.

This is what that can sound like:

- **Fear-based leader 1:** "My town car barely made it into your garage downstairs. I don't know how you get work done with so little

space in this office. Our headquarters is two million square feet."
- **Fear-based leader 2:** "Our headquarters is small because we have five massive data centers that house our billions of users' data off site. Everything is optimized, and we know almost everything about almost anyone in the world. We still did a massive RIF last month, and now we have even more capital to run things."
- **Fear-based leader 3:** "That's nice—but I hope you know you can't get that done without our funding. SoftBank just gave us $4 billion and I think we'll have that deployed by the end of this year."

In this script, you can see two things: First, they're all trying to sound like they're *the biggest*, and *the baddest*. Second, you can see *what they value*. Leader 1 is old school—he equates physical size with might. Leader 2 is about applied intelligence, and ruthlessness. Leader 3 wants people to know that he has the others in a noose, by the purse strings—the language he speaks in is money.

They are also all *talking over one another* in a *free-for-all for control*. Posturing is not about power. It's about managing perception. The loudest, biggest, and most intimidating person in the room is often the most insecure. They bluff not because they are strong, but because they are afraid. This dialogue *screams*, "I'm afraid!"

A *strengths-based leader* only postures if they have to interact with a *strongman*—someone whose respect language is coded to only understand posturing. Because they are *strengths-based*, they are *flexible*—and that means that they are *adaptable* in their communications—they could greet leader 1 in terms of physical space, leader 2 with something intelligent, and leader 3 by talking about their mutual interest in resources.

If they were in a room with all three of them together, the strengths-based leader would make a conscious choice whether to defuse the posturing, play them off each other, or assume control of the dialogue, because their communication is *strategic*, not *fear-based*.

If you wanted to defuse, that could sound like:

> "I brought you here because you are all the best of the best in your fields. John, you are a master at operating in the physical world, James, your company uses information to make truly informed choices, and Jack, you bring the capital to make it happen. I couldn't do this without each of you, and you are truly titans. Now, let's get down to brass tacks." *This strokes all their egos to calm them down.*

If you wanted to play them off each other, that might sound like:

> "Wow, really, I heard James did a share buyback to finance his next set of data centers, and that Jack said remote work was the wave of the future." *This suggests to Jack that his money/strength is not valued, while telling John that he's as irrelevant as he fears in his older age.*

If you wanted to assume control of the dialogue, that might sound like:

> "Your time is deeply valuable, so let's get to it: Can James buy John's land for a data center using Jack's capital?" *This gives them a direction that all three care about, while validating their need for self-importance.*

If you work under a fear-based leader, what strategies can you use to defuse their posturing? If you are a leader yourself, how can you recognize the 4F types around you, and create trust instead?

Secret Tests: They're Grading You

You're secretly being graded every time you interact with a fear-based leader, because in their quest for dominance, they bucket people into two camps: weak sheep, and useful tools. But this happens most critically in the first few interactions.

You need to realize that you are being evaluated, so that you get the grade that allows you to have the impact that you want to have, or are able to keep the power you'd like to amass or retain.

So be on your guard—the first five times a fear-based leader is interacting with you, they are *testing* you. Not in the sense of a literal quiz, but they are probing you to understand:

1. How much can they push you around?

2. How smart are you?
3. Do you understand power dynamics?
4. Is your head spun by crazy making?

It's important that you *recognize these tests* for what they are, *and respond in a strategic way.*

First, they may try an end run around rules or limits—doing something illegal in front of you, or to you, to see if you object. If you want to be seen as a pushover and underestimated, let them. If you want them to know you're watching them and aren't afraid, call them out. If you want to be careful—to let them know you're watching, but not going to be oppositional—you call it out in the guise of *looking out for them.* "Hey, I want to make sure you're aware that this opens the door to legal exposure—if we want to fire 20 percent of the staff, the smart way to do it is . . ." This says, "I'm watching, I see you, and I know how to navigate the system to make it yours."

Then, they might try blustering in front of you. They may say things that are not true, and posture to make themselves as big and scary as possible ("I'm going to take this company private if our shareholders don't stop bothering me. Every analyst on the street is worthless. Only I know how to keep the trains running in a visionary way. Visionaries like me only come once in a generation").

If you look scared, you fail the test. If you call them out ("That's insane, you can't do that"), you become an enemy. If you join in ("No shit, we're lucky to have you; I've never met an industry analyst that couldn't be bribed"), then you are a temporary ally. *They want to know if you're a real opponent.*

Then, they may try crazy making. *Crazy making* means *distorting reality around someone until they can no longer tell what's true*. It's deliberately generating hazy fluff that makes it hard for you to remember what is real.

Let's say that the fear-based leader had someone in IT spy on you, report your every move, and leak data from private correspondence. If you call them out, the leader might say, "*You're* the one who's spying on *me*. You can't be trusted. Stop this immediately, or I'll fire you." If you *let* them brand you like this, they know that they can *spin your head*, and that they can *get away with targeting you by distorting your reality.*

Ninety percent of people *fail their tests* and are deemed incompetent, beneath them, and manipulable. The trick is to call the bullshit, or go along with the bullshit, in the ways that are *advantageous to you*, and establish you as someone who is: 1) awake and 2) as smart as, or smarter than, they are.

You want them to see you as someone who *understands their world* but is not a *threat to their power*, so that they think twice about stepping on you—either because you know how to help them, because they think you're powerless, or because you have shown teeth.

Your goal isn't to win their loyalty, because they are loyal to no one but themselves. It's to position yourself in a way that keeps you in control of your own role and influence. Whether you want to be underestimated, seen as a useful strategist, or marked as untouchable, how you navigate these early tests determines your standing in their world.

It can be positive to be underestimated, but if you're seen as totally worthless, you will not have a seat at the table to influence the decisions you care most about. You need to be seen as being able to be on their wavelength, with an active mind, or they will classify you as a sheep. If you're a sheep, they will not hesitate to slaughter you.

Clocking and Tailoring to Emotional Maturity Levels: They're Not Really Adults

Many adults that you see are not actual adults. This is because a lot of people do not get the support they need growing up to fully mature into nuanced, responsible people who take full ownership of themselves.

Sure, they might pay their taxes—but inside, they're *emotionally stunted*, and their *body age* does not match their *emotional age*. This is especially true of adults who experienced neglect or trauma as children.

To some degree, society recognizes this—you may hear people say things like, "Steve is eighty, but he never grew up, I swear, he acts just like my five-year-old!" Or, "It feels like everything at my work is like I'm back in high school; everyone is so cliquey, I wish people would grow up already!"

The *emotional age* of the people around you is critical to understand, because it determines how they act in all forms of communication, and how they make decisions—decisions that likely *impact you.*

An emotionally mature adult will make choices based on all available information, their or their organization's values, and the needs of themselves or the people around them. An emotionally immature person will make choices based on *impulse* to satisfy *base needs*, with no concept of how anyone else around them will be impacted.

No fear-based leader is an emotional adult. Even if they're a genius—a person can have a PhD, run a billion-dollar company, and still throw tantrums like a toddler when they don't get their way.

So, it is *critical* that you learn to clock their age, so that you understand what motivates them. If you know what *motivates* them, then you can *influence* them to protect the things that, as an adult, they should care about.

Here's a quick chart that can help you identify the *real* age of the people around you.

Side note: If the chart looks like a negative characterization of children, remember that emotionally immature adults retain the *negative developmental-stage aspects* of children, but *not their sweetness or innocence.*

Behaviors	Emotional age
Resource guarding, easily bored, distractible, low distress tolerance, says no to things just because they can, throws all-caps tantrums	2 years old
Obsessed with playground dynamics, building the biggest tower/rocket/house/valuation, wants to be liked but has trouble sharing, easily jealous, has shallow, transient relationships	5 years old
Sophomoric humor, lack of understanding of consequences of actions, high level of shallow interests in things like sports, history, transportation	8 years old
Obsessed with image, acting out roles (wife, mother, hero, protector), petty, gossipy, limited to no ability to communicate or discuss emotions	Teenager

Let's practice. Here are four statements of executives that closely map to things I've heard in real life.

Example 1: "Jamie will *not stop* trying to mentor me but I am totally competent in my work and *I don't need a mentor.* But she thinks she needs to *mother me* and someone told her she needs to *mentor people* to get promoted, so she won't stop doing this because she wants to *boost her image.*"

The clues: Jamie is *playing pretend roles* regardless of whether the people around her want to play house—or in this case, mentor/mother—with her, and she is obsessed with her image.
The answer: She's an emotional teenager.

Example 2: "I'm going to build the largest data center this world has ever seen. People need to understand that tech founders are the innovative emperors of the data age, but John and David are idiots for not wanting to build with me, I'm cutting them out of this project."

The clues: This person wants to build the biggest thing, sees himself in simplified, delusional terms (an emperor), and is upset that the other billionaires won't play with him, so he cuts them out of the shallow relationship he had.
The answer: This person is an emotional five-year-old.

Example 3: "Our company WILL NOT TOLERATE leakers to the press. ANYONE WHO LEAKS IS A DISLOYAL

SHILL. No, I will not be giving people bonuses this year! By the way, did you see the bonus that Goldman gave us for signing on?"

The clues: This person is throwing a tantrum, saying no just because they can, and is easily distracted by a mention of bonuses.
The answer: This person is an emotional two-year-old.

So what does this mean for you? You need to always, always, speak to the person in terms of their *emotional age*.

With Jamie, in example one, the person could say, "Jamie, I heard this really cool team over here needs your help with their code QA, and the new hire who joined yesterday seems so confused. Do you think you could help save the first team, and mentor the other?" This appeals to Jamie's sense of *belonging* and desire to join the *it crowd* while giving her someone she is *allowed to save and mother*.

With example two, the direct report could say to the billionaire, "You're right, they are total dummies for not wanting to get in on this. Your data center is going to be the best data center." This appeals to the billionaire's need for *reassurance* that he is *liked and loved*, which is what most five-year-olds really want.

With example three, you might say, "Yeah, that was a great bonus you got for us! Here's the coffee you asked for, and a bagel. Would you like to fly out to your cabin at Jackson Hole tonight? You work so hard, you deserve a break." This 1) validates their baby ego, 2) addresses that two-year-old tantrums are usually because they are hungry, tired, or bored, and 3) gives them a way out of the stifling corporate environment that is way too buttoned up and nuanced for a two-year-old. People like this need frequent distraction, a lot of coddling, a lot of validation, and plenty of time for breaks, food, naps, and "playtime" with other leaders or their sycophants.

So how old, really, are the people around you?

Outdated Models: They're Out of Date

Now that you understand that fear-based leaders are really their *emotional age*, not body age, it unlocks an understanding of something else: They don't have the capacity to grow. They don't have the capacity to change, mature, or learn. They do not improve with time.

This is frustrating, but it's also a good thing—because it makes them a known quantity. They run the same tired playbook over and over. Bluster, intimidate, threaten, posture, gaslight.

And, it opens them up to a vulnerability in their thinking.

They don't grow—so they assume you don't, either.

This means they are almost always operating with old information. They assume you are always the you that they first met, even if that was many years ago—because they do not change, even as their body ages.

This means that you can *run circles around them* and they won't be any the wiser. It means that you can *intentionally create* your first impression to *be what you want* and then grow, change, develop, or actually be something very different.

The place where people see this most often is families, so that's the example I will use initially. Imagine Jo, a thoughtful, quiet, shy child who is always reading, and loves to bake. Adults around her dismiss her as being irrelevant because she's quiet, think that all she cares about is books, not the world around her, and write her off as being excessively domestic, and obsessed with sweets. This makes her a *known, nonintimidating factor* to be dismissed.

When it's fifteen years later, and Jo has her master's from an Ivy League school, and is working as a policy analyst, those fear-based adults who knew her as a child will likely still ask her: 1) what she is reading and 2) what recipes she's baked lately, then ignore her at all events.

While this is insulting, it means that Jo has *freedom*. She can go truly be whatever she wants to be, and the fear-based people around her will always see the same one-dimensional, cardboard cutout of who she was years ago.

This means several things:

1. Your first impressions around a fear-based leader matter.

2. You can use those impressions to your advantage.
3. You are shielded by the cardboard cutout version of yourself.

Most people spend years trying to convince fear-based leaders to update their perception. They get caught up in the frustration of not being seen and known. They don't realize that it provides strategic cover and an open license.

So instead, decide: In the first three months around a leader like this, how do you want to play it? You can be seen as intelligent but submissive, calm and stoic, an attack dog to be sicced on others, or any other number of things that could be useful to you. Be a nonthreatening sleeper agent! Be seen as a tool!

Then, what do you *actually* want to be? Do you want to be a witness to the fear-based leader's regime? Do you want to work against it? Do you want to protect certain teams, projects, or assets?

Your power comes not from correcting them, but from knowing that there is agency waiting for you behind the outdated assumptions.

The Vulnerabilities of the Arrogant: They Have Big Blind Spots

You understand now that fear-based leaders do not grow, or believe others can grow. But you may not realize that they are also *blind*.

What do I mean? Well, fear-based leaders are *incredibly arrogant*. You can tell, because they will often say things like, "I'm right 99 percent of the time"; "I'm a once-in-a-generation intellect"; "People should be grateful to have a design genius like me in charge"; "I'm the Iron Man of my industry."

As soon as someone becomes arrogant, blinders start to cloud their vision. They start looking for *confirmation* of their *gut feelings* rather than keeping an ear to the ground in reality. They start wanting to be surrounded by people who say, "Yes, yes, yes. Yes, you are special. Yes, you are the best. Yes, you are the center of this universe."

They end up surrounded by sycophants and yes-men, who all want a piece of their power and constantly reinforce whatever serves them the most.

The farther the leader's bubble gets from the real world, and the more yes-men who insulate them, the more *distorted* their view of reality gets. Eventually, they become *blind*.

Why? Arrogant people don't look very closely. They assume everyone around them is incredibly impressed. Especially the people who nod, smile, and bring them coffee. *This is their first mistake—and it gives you latitude to play.*

Arrogant people are also *micromanagers*. They think that no team can make progress without their particular input. But their organizations are usually too big for them to effectively see what's happening in every section, all the time.

Arrogant people also think that anyone around them who is friendly, feminine, and young is weak. They will underestimate anyone who shows softness or inclusivity. Case in point: When I was a consultant, in male-dominated industries like industrial aerospace engineering, we would send in young women to get male employees in their fifties—who saw them as cute daughters—to spill their guts to an attentive, nonthreatening audience, so that we could actually figure out where the issues were and recommend strategic changes.

Their confidence can be convincing. Don't let it fool you—I have seen many, many people like this who say, "I'm always right," who are actually making incorrect statements more than 80 percent of the time. One hundred percent assuredness is actually a **warning sign**. It is a warning that someone is not open minded to the fact that there are *variables outside of their control.*

People think that arrogant leaders are dominant because they're smarter, more competent, or have better instincts. In reality, their arrogance is a liability—it makes them easy to manipulate.

So what does this mean for you? *Play the edges of their arrogant ignorance.* Nod along—they are not used to people questioning them and will assume that you are convinced. Get a front seat to their mistakes, so that you are ready to cut them down when the time comes—there is always someone bigger you can sell them out to.

Once you do, then your role flips, because that person will see you as ruthless and cunning, someone whose loyalty is for sale . . . and then the process begins again, this time as a confidant.

Playing Realities: They're Not in Reality

Now let's level up: You understand that these types of leaders don't grow, and are blind with arrogance and full-out outdated assumptions.

What you may not have realized yet is that they are also often *not functioning in the same reality.*

While it can be counterintuitive to understand, people exist on a continuum in their ability to accurately absorb the events around them. The more insecure someone is, often, the more unhelpful filters they have on their perception. For example, someone who has often been bullied may think, "The world is out to get me. Nowhere is safe." Therefore they may be unable to realize when they are in environments where they *are* safe.

This can be hard to process, because most people assume they process reality accurately, and that others do, too. If you're self-aware, you assume others are. If you wouldn't knowingly deceive yourself or others, you assume others wouldn't, either. *This is incorrect. If you think this way, it will hobble you in navigating power dynamics.* These types of leaders *do not make decisions based on logic, or facts,* but their *fears, insecurities, and inaccurate reads of reality.* If you assume people are making decisions based on the same reality you see, you'll miscalculate their actions—and the things you care most about will be lost. The higher the stakes, the more dangerous that assumption becomes.

Where this comes into play with leadership and organizations is in something most people do *not* understand: that people can engage in *collective denials of reality.* These are *protective mechanisms* that allow people to *insulate themselves* when the truth hurts. In a family system, twenty people may collectively perpetuate the myth that "we're one big happy family; we all had a great childhood," so they don't have to admit that no one likes each other and the family has a history of abuse. In a *business system,* people might all tell each other, "We're the most elite firm on the street; we're the model who everyone else is based on," when really, the company is run extremely poorly, and it's struggling to succeed. In a *political system,* a group may say, "We're the only party who cares about the forgotten poor," when really, they only care about certain sections of society.

This can play out in very strange ways. In one case, I was speaking with someone who has had a very hard life. She was only able to engage in shallow discussions—things like the weather, or pets. Beyond that, she'd get overwhelmed. Everything else bounced. This led to conversations like this:

> **Friend:** "How are you doing, Kate?"
>
> **Me:** "I'm dealing with some serious health issues; it has been very tough."
>
> **Friend:** "I'm so glad things are going perfectly well. I will tell all our friends that you are doing great and are happy and healthy."

She could not *absorb* what I was saying, because in her mind, she needs to protect that all her friends are *happy, healthy, and safe*, because to think otherwise would mean that the *world is more dangerous than she can tolerate.*

Another time I saw this play out was in a group meeting. I got to the meeting on time, and the facilitator and I started to work. Then, two other participants arrived, and the facilitator said, "Hey, I need you both to arrive on time in the future. Please respect that all our time is valuable." The other participants said: "You're being so rude to us! Did you just see her be mean to me?" "We're paying you so much money and we can show up whenever we want! We're leaving."

In that example, they engaged in the collective reality

that *they are good and can do no wrong*, which meant that the *facilitator was bad*. Their egos were protecting them from the fact that *their actions have consequences* and that their irresponsible behavior *negatively impacts others*.

People who engage in collective denials of reality are constantly defending against threats to their awareness—so people who *disrupt* the reality are seen as *dangerous* to the denial equilibrium, and are therefore targeted. People will defend their *self-perception* more aggressively than their *actual interests*.

Because fear-based leaders are *deeply insecure* and *surround themselves with sycophants*, they are often *not living in a fact-based reality*.

This means they're making decisions based on stories, not facts. If you understand the story they've built, you can predict what they'll do next—and, if you're careful, you can shape it. The trick is to *study their delusions* so that you can *influence the choices they make*.

When you are in meetings with a fear-based leader, pay close attention to what they're able to process and absorb, and what bounces off. They will often latch on to certain facts or pieces of information, and ignore the rest. *Catalog what they are ignoring.* What patterns can you see? If those things are mentioned later, do they ignore them a second time? Do they act like they've never been told those things before?

Pay attention to what they repeat. People who exist outside of reality constantly have to reinforce their worldview against the facts coming in. Leaders might say, "We're a best-in-class org and we need other people to get in line" five times in the same meeting. They might say, "I'm the only one who can solve this problem because you numbskulls can't do this without me."

For the first example, the leader is saying, "We are the example from whom all others should flow, and other people are not respecting our dominance." This means that you could likely attack other companies/entities that are working against your own goals, in the name of defending the dominance of your leader.

In the second example, the leader is saying, "No one is capable of getting work done without me." Okay, well, if you don't like their initiatives, *stop all work except when they are present.* Play into their belief by telling them it's impossible for you to get work done without getting every single tiny step approved by them. *This will slow their progress and stop bad initiatives from taking place.* They may be micromanagers, but they only have twenty-four hours in a day. *Play into the fact that they think they are indispensable.*

Who around you seems to be allergic to facts? How can you turn that to your advantage?

Forgive and Forget Is for Fools: They Have Long Memories

Forgive and forget is for fools . . . is what fear-based leaders think. Even if they pretend to, they never forget a slight. They think that holding on to hate gives them strength to strike and crush—when really, it is the protective mechanism that keeps the pain of not being loved as children from breaking through to their consciousness.

Just like how once you enter a fear-based leader's circle, they believe you "belong" to them forever, if you cross them, you end up with a direct one-way ticket to their blacklist.

It doesn't matter if you have served them loyally for decades, or if 90 percent of your behavior is supportive— if even 10 percent is in opposition, and you're discovered, your actions become a source of vengeance. They may *pretend* to forgive you—but believe me, in their mind, they are still seething.

This emphasis on revenge can feel strange to people who want to let bygones be bygones, and live happy, resilient lives. But it comes from zero-sum thinking—just like when someone says, "No one helped me when I was going through school; why should I bother helping you?" They think that because they have felt pain, others deserve to feel it too—*particularly* people who surface their sense of shame (usually stemming from losing face, or public defeat).

They will do anything to smother the shame when they feel it rising—to keep it from being pulled forward again. It feels like complete anathema to them—you could almost think of it as an "allergic reaction." Except, when they start to choke in a shame spiral, they don't use an EpiPen—they smash the button that launches their irritant into exile.

This is demonstrated really clearly in *Star Wars*, where those who bring bad news (or defiance) to Darth Vader and Kylo Ren are immediately choked to death. To them, that feels proportionate—because when they feel shame, or get a waft of failure, it feels to them *like they're dying*. It feels like a *natural defense* to kill the thing that's *threatening their life*. Except, in reality, their life isn't in danger; it just *feels* like it. So, to the people around them, it seems like obsessive, off-the-handle reactions.

They also believe that they need hatred in order to stay in motion. They see it as fuel for their fire. But they don't understand that running on hate is essentially like trying to keep a fire kindled by solely burning straw. It lights up quick, and makes a big flame, but it's not very intense, very hot, or very sustaining. It burns out easily, and so they constantly have to feed their fire with more enemies, more opposition, more distraction.

When they're on the defensive, and can convince themselves that they are under attack, they avoid being still, avoid feeling the feelings underneath the irascible anger that would consume them, should they ever be left alone with themselves. Were that to happen, they would be left with utter emptiness, and the knowledge that they have never been loved unconditionally and have never been truly known. That pain is too much for them to manage.

So, if you want to operate in their ecosystems, pay very close attention to what they consider a slight—and try to stay off of their shit list. Feed your personal fire with purpose, meaning, and community, not hate. If you cannot avoid occasionally crossing them, then do everything you can to be useful. If you're needed, and hard to replace, there's less of a chance that you'll be written off entirely in the short term. But, in the long term—once you're an enemy, there's no going back.

It Will Never Be Me: Tactics Work Predictably on Them

You might ask why I would give you a playbook to deal with these people. If I tell you all the secret ways to manage them, won't they wise up, making the advice null and void?

The answer is no—they won't.

First, no one wants to associate themselves with being "fear-based." To sound like your behavior is motivated by fear, or that you motivate through fear, is not something most people will willingly claim.

But even if someone marched into a room and said, "I am going to be the new age Machiavelli! Fear me or forever regret your choices," their arrogance means that they believe that they are *exceptional*, even though they are *deeply unoriginal*. They think, "These strategies might work on lesser mortals—but they will never work on *me*."

This plays out in funny ways when you look at the structures surrounding fear-based leaders. Very often, the people who are directly beneath them on the pyramid joined or rose through the ranks seeing the leader treat the people around them like trash—but the voice in their head said, *"I'm special.* Of course they'd never treat *me* in such a way." By the time the leader discards them like the meaningless accessory they are, it's too late, and the wake-up is painful.

For the leaders themselves to admit that they are a fear-based leader, which is to say truly abhorrent, they would have to absorb the totality of the abusive actions that they have undertaken in their lifetime and their collective impact—and remorse is one of the most painful things someone can ever experience.

People will spend *years* dancing around truths like two poles of a magnet, because facing what is real and true is way, way too much for them. I know, because I was taught at my father's knee to *be* a fear-based leader, and until I had enough support to learn other ways of being, I instinctively avoided internalizing the impact of my actions, too.

When I finally realized how much harm this way of being—even behaving at just an increment of the intensity of the people I had learned it from—had caused, it was the single most devastating realization of my life, and I spent the next many years studying deeply to ensure that I would never inadvertently hurt anyone else ever again.

So don't worry—even if your bosses or adversaries read this book, they're unlikely to notice if you use these tactics on them.

Key Takeaways and Reflection Questions

Takeaways

1. Fear-based leaders are driven by fear and shame, and this is what they use to motivate others. This is an ineffective strategy.
2. Reactions are impulses, and responses are intentional. The goal is to always respond, not react.
3. Fear-based leaders posture to manage perceptions as part of fight responses. See through their bluster to the insecurity underneath.
4. Fear-based leaders constantly test and monitor to detect vulnerabilities. Pass their tests to retain control of your domain.
5. Most fear-based leaders are not emotional adults. You need to meet them at their emotional age.

6. Because fear-based leaders don't grow, they assume you won't, either. Embrace being underestimated.
7. Fear-based leaders are deeply arrogant, which means they have big blind spots that leave them open to being influenced.
8. Fear-based leaders exist in their own realities, with alternate, emotionally driven fact bases. Understanding what stories make it into their reality creates lanes to upwardly manage them.
9. Fear-based leaders are petty, with long memories. Once you cross them, you're on their blacklist forever.
10. Because of their arrogance, tactics work highly predictably on them.

Reflection Questions

1. How do the leaders around you motivate others—out of fear, or out of intrinsic motivation?
2. How much of the time do you react, versus respond?
3. What emotional age are the leaders around you?
4. What narratives do you hear the fear-based leaders in your life telling themselves and the world?

Part Two

The Tool Kit: Specific Strategies for How to Thrive Under Fear-Based Authoritarian Leaders

Send in the Clowns, They're Already Here:[1] How to Upwardly Manage Fear-Based Leaders

Okay, so now that you're *in the mind* of a fear-based leader and understand their win/loss mindset, what can you actually do about it?

First, you need to decide if you want to stay, or if you want to leave. If you want to stay in the organization that now has an impulsive cretin at the top because you think it will help your customers, patients, or users, that's a valid choice. If you want to leave to find a place that better reflects your values, that's fine, too—but know that this wave of leadership is sweeping across the public, private,

---

1. Reference to song by Judy Collins and Steven Sondheim.

and social sectors right now, so it may be like looking for a needle in a haystack.

If you're staying, you need to batten down the hatches, then get down and dirty with tactics of your own.

First, you need to understand what these people *trade in*. In order to *manipulate*, these types of leaders need one thing above all else: information.

With that in mind:

Rule #1: Do not, under any circumstances, give them **any information about what you care about**. These types of leaders don't use carrots—they use sticks. You might think it's innocuous to tell them how much you love going to your kid's Little League games—until they make you miss every one for a month because you failed to anticipate their needs closely enough. To them, *caring about anything is weak*—and the more you show your humanity, the less they'll tolerate you. So, don't mention pets, kids, family, hobbies—if it's not related to money, power, or your direct work, **keep it off the table**. When it comes to your actual work, do not show passion or energy about any particular initiative—unless it's one that they currently favor.

Rule #2: If you want something approved, **always let it be their idea**. Trickle bottom-up facts that paint a contextual picture, then feign that you *don't know what to do about it*. Make the fact pattern so obvious that there is *no other conclusion than the one that you want*. When they pick the path you want, *be thankful* and say, "Oh my gosh, I totally didn't think of that. I'm so glad that you're here."

Rule #3: When in doubt, **stroke their ego**. Tell them how glad you are that someone competent is finally in the room. Tell them what a nightmare it was to be surrounded by people obsessed with rules and doing the right thing. This gets them *to let their guard down.*

Rule #4: Encourage **monologuing**. People like this love to go on harangues—about how they've been wronged, about how hard their life is, about other people's inadequacies. This can be hard to stomach at first, but it helps you *learn more about their thinking* so that you either *catch them doing/saying illegal things* or notice areas where they are about to make major mistakes that will blow back in their face—that you may be able to *help blow up in their face.* As long as your signature isn't on one of those initiatives and it can't be traced back to you, *do it.*

Rule #5: Learn to **love being underestimated**. When people like this don't think you're capable, they treat you like you're an ugly vase in the room. If they think you're weak, beta, passive, or ineffectual, *you become invisible.* When you're *invisible*, you have *much more freedom* about what and when you do things that are important to you.

Rule #6: Study their triggers in order to learn how to **bait and distract them** (toddler skills 101). Every time you see them have a major emotional reaction, *write it down.* What happened, and what was their response? This way you have a list: trigger A → monologuing for twenty minutes, trigger B → explosion, and so on. This effectively creates a list of your buttons—if you're in a meeting and you want something to fall off the agenda, *trigger a* *twenty-minute monologue in the last ten minutes.* If you need them to forget what they're doing so that a major priority doesn't get axed, *trigger an explosion.* But the trick is, *the trigger always has to be attributed to someone not you.* E.g., "I was talking to Risha and she said our VP of marketing told her you have no idea what you're doing. I immediately told her that was ridiculous, but I just wanted to let you know you're being undermined." *This establishes you as loyal, while setting off the trigger.*

Rule #7: Validate their fragile feelings. Remember they are insecure, immature people, so even though you'll want to do the opposite, *be compassionate.* Frequently validate their feelings to earn their trust, which will earn you freedom and influence. As much as it might kill you, this sounds like, "That must be so hard. Wow, no one understands you, do they? Why can't we just get it faster? Ugh, we're the worst."

Rule #8: Find ways to **make them look good**, so you're seen as useful and are kept around. In a system of alphas and betas, the *number one thing* a beta can do is push an alpha farther up the pedestal. You won't be appreciated, but you won't be axed, either.

Sweat Them with Silence: Availability Is Leverage

If you ever want to torture a fear-based leader, or gain leverage over them, *don't be available.*

This does a few things:

1. It undercuts their belief that they are important and entitled to your time, which angers them and makes them feel more insecure.
2. It triggers a cascade of *stories.*
3. It plays into their paranoia.
4. It gives them the absence of an opponent.

There have been times where I've won major negotiations *simply by not replying for a week.* That sounds counterintuitive, right?

Here's how it works.

First, when you're not immediately available, it says to them you're not paying the respect that they're due. Doubt starts to creep into their mind.

Their overactive, insecure brains start generating a million reasons why you might be messing with them. That might sound like, "Anna must be plotting against me. She's giving me the silent treatment so that I back off on my resource requests. She is likely spending the time organizing the other direct reports into a coalition against my demands. I bet she's too stupid to realize how smart I am and the respect that I'm owed."

The stories then start turning into paranoia. "What if Anna doesn't really support me, but is just pretending to? What if they all don't really see me as a leader, but as a dork? What if when I go to work tomorrow, they all laugh at me?"

This then starves them of 1) a tool, 2) a punching bag, 3) an opponent, and 4) a supply of attention.

They don't actually like work, so they need *tools* to do their bidding.

They need to constantly shore up their superiority so their ego does not collapse, which means they need *punching bags* to demean and step on to remain on their pedestal.

They need constant *conflict* as a source of energy, because their internal world is full of aggressive pushing and pulling, and they need the space around them to be as off balance as they feel.

And they need a *fawn*, someone to tell them how

great they are, and listen to them monologue about how they think they are exceptional geniuses, because in their minds they are kings who always deserve an audience.

So the best way to get to them is not to fight back—it feeds them and brings them energy to be in conflict—it's to simply *wait an extra day to reply.*

This strategy needs titration—it can cause them to bluster more, or to blow up—but it also shows strength, because it suggests that you have boundaries, and are immune to their reactive tactics, without any show of defiance.

Let them spiral. Let them think the worst. Then come back, stroke their ego, and tell them everything's okay. *This messes with them more than anything else—because it makes them feel unstable to a degree they can't admit.* This is because fear-based leaders hate being alone, because it makes them spend time with someone they hate: themselves.

Painting in Gray in a Black-and-White World: Embrace Nuance

Fear-based leaders think in black and white. Mature, strengths-based leaders paint in shades of gray.

Imagine that as you walk through the world, everyone around you is covered in totally white or totally black paint. Everything that you touch leaves smudges of white or black. But if you, with your pristine white canvas, get a speck of black on you, then flip! You're now all black, too.

This is how a fear-based leader sees the world. Everyone is *all good* or *all bad* with zero nuance. If that sounds simplistic and immature, it is. It's a shallow way of seeing things.

It makes them act in unusual but predictable ways. The first rule for them: Their *own* canvas must always be a sparkling, clean bright white. Not a *single drop* of black paint can touch them, or their canvas is *ruined forever.*

This means that they will do almost anything to avoid being painted with a black brush. They will run from responsibility, ownership, or awareness of the consequences of their actions and choices. They will blame or step on anyone else around them. They will always think that any bad thing happening to them is someone else's fault.

Why? Because if they think that people can only be a hero or a villain, they cannot *tolerate* a narrative in which they are the bad guy in a story. It's anathema to their insecure hearts, and completely ego dystonic. It's like if every day of your life, you told yourself over and over you were a saint to rival Mother Teresa, and then one day, someone turns up and tells you that you've been the devil all along. It might sound laughable—but if your *entire sense of self-worth* is built on being a hero/cowboy/rescuer and then something contradicts that, it causes immense distress and pain.

This is why trying to give a leader like this an analysis of complex trade-offs rarely ever works. To them, there is only the right choice or the wrong choice, the strong choice or the weak choice, the good thing or the bad thing.

Instead, when you need them to do something that you want, *show them how it fits into their hero narrative.* "I bet people would totally nominate you for our industry award if you go down path A."

And, be very, very careful about suggesting that anything is their fault. Do not put them in the same sentence as one that suggests a mistake. Even if it was totally their issue, and nothing else could possibly have caused the mess, omit pronouns, e.g., "It seems that path A was taken and that it caused some issues."

If you *do* throw some black paint on their canvas, prepare for them to go absolutely postal. I have seen people fire their closest colleagues and acolytes, blacklist former close friends as enemies, and cut off contact with people that they have had *decades* of relationships with, overnight, with no warning. All of this was for reasons perceived as petty slights ("Anna suggested that I made a bad decision; I'll *show her a bad decision*"). If it's a choice between you and their self-concept, you will never win.

Starve the Dragon: Put Them on an Attention Diet

Imagine your leader as a massive, hulking dragon, with plumes of smoke coming out of their snout.

Except instead of feeding on fleeing townspeople, this dragon feeds on *attention*. Not just *good* attention—any type of reaction related to an action they took works. This is why these types of leaders have a love/hate relationship with the press—it's attention, but not the kind they can control. It's why so many buy newspaper companies—so that they *can* control it.

They love nothing more than shouting "Boo!" and watching someone jump.

So the number one skill, over anything else that you need to learn to survive them, is a poker face. You need a face so boring, so inert, so blank, calm, or beatific that their eyes glaze over, as if you are part of the wallpaper.

Some people call this *gray rocking*. Because if a dragon flies overhead, you want them to see you as part of the landscape—a gray rock.

When they are getting under your skin, and making you really steamed, remember: That is what they want. Your indignation is jet fuel for their ego. The smart choice is to be opaque. Let their claws slide off of your smooth, glassy surface, finding no purchase.

Note: This requires *complete consistency*. Any time you break your stoic character, you start back over. Rather than learning that you're boring, they've learned your breaking point.

At first when you start trying this, they will rage against you for being *boring*, for being lifeless, for being dull, for acting like "a lump." Ignore this. Let them get bored. They may try to shout at you, to essentially kick you into reacting. They may actually throw things at the wall. Remember that *a rock cannot be harmed by a shout. A rock cannot be harmed by someone throwing all their budget reports across the room.* This is a temporary test to see if they can get you to jump back into a dysfunctional dance of reactions. Once they realize you won't rise to it, they will either switch to wooing you, or find a different target.

Typically, the more distance—emotional or physical—you put between yourself and a fear-based leader, the more they will return to their "best behavior" to try to win you back into their chaotic embrace. Only be as close as you need to be to get the things you need done completed. Try to make that distance reasonably far, so that rather than using you as a punching bag, they're always just trying to lure you a little closer, by putting on their sweet-as-honey guise. This is right where you want them to be—needing to behave in order to have you dangling like an attention carrot on a stick in front of them. *Be the carrot.* When they get a little too close, take a step farther back. When they back away, take one step closer again.

By manipulating their *supply of attention*, you *manipulate them while showing strength.*

Move Fast and Break Things:[1] Destruction Is the Point

Okay, now you understand that what fear-based leaders want most is attention. The biggest, most interesting forms of attention come as a *reaction*.

This is why you can't share any information about what you care about with them—because they will then use that as leverage to get a reaction, sometimes by giving you that thing (e.g., PTO without being on call), and sometimes by taking it away (making you work through your vacation).

Positive reactions only feed them for so long—like a sugar high. *Negative reactions* feed them for weeks—because when they see the explosions they can cause, it makes them *feel powerful.*

---

1. Term coined by Facebook.

This is where we get to a concept called "move fast and break things." This is a common business phrase in the tech industry. In its initial form, it meant to prioritize rapid innovation and experimentation, even if that means occasionally causing disruption or making mistakes, with the idea that quick progress is more important than playing it safe and moving slowly. That's well and fine (even if building intentional infrastructure may be better).

However, there is a *new version* of this phrase that has an entirely different meaning. In the context of fear-based leaders, it means not breaking things by accident through speed, but *breaking things on purpose as fast as possible.*

This may be really foreign to you—you may be a builder, not a destroyer.

Fear-based leaders are not like you.

They *don't care* if they're destroying something that can't be rebuilt. They *don't care* if it's costly, and they *don't care* who else is impacted.

They *only care about getting a reaction from you.* Breaking things rapidly keeps opponents in a defensive, reactive state.

If someone comes into your house while you're asleep, lights a fire, and you then have to spend the next five months mired in insurance, trying to find a place to sleep, and replacing all your possessions, then you have been *handled.*

You are *livid*, which makes the arsonist feel *powerful*, and you are stuck in a *survival state*, which means you cannot effectively *resist.*

The key is understanding that in business in the past, this phrase has meant positive *disruption*. In a fear-based leadership context, which is based on a *feudal sense of conquering*, it means *destruction*.

You need to be *ready* for *major things to be destroyed overnight*. I have seen fear-based leaders kill fledgling companies, tear up ten months of work out of spite, and engage in crisis PR or lawsuits just because they can.

Sometimes, if they can't have something, they want *no one to be able to have it*. They would rather *rule a ruin* than have something *intact exist outside their control*.

Outline what's actually most important to you. Have a plan to hide and protect it. *Then give them false targets.* Let slip what's "important" to you, so that they take the bait and destroy that, instead.

Set contingency plans. Back up important files. Have an emergency fund with at least four months of expenses, some of it offshore if possible. Always have a résumé prepared. Do four networking calls a month. Read the section in part three about how to pitch and select lawyers. If you think you need to, retain employment-law counsel in advance.

I Own You: You Are a Possession

Something that is important to understand about these types of people is that they subscribe to a more primitive notion of power—so primitive, in fact, that it takes us back to the Middle Ages. In a healthy place of work or system, each person is their own person—free agents, you might say. If someone doesn't like something, they can make the choice to leave. That is not how things work with fear-based leaders. Once you're a part of their organization, you're in it for life—even if you think you've left.

Every fear-based leader secretly has a vision of themself as a feudal lord, complete with the retinue associated with that position. To them, every person below them on the hierarchy is a peasant, as uneducated and powerless as that status implies. If you are someone who works for them, you owe them *fealty*. Not loyalty, which is different, and derives from positive respect and association, but *fealty*. *Fealty* means that you pledge your entire being to the "lord"—that you would die for them, or in this case, go to jail, commit illegal acts, cover up unsavory nonsense, and so on.

Knights for such a lord swear a *lifetime duty*—and that's what they expect of you. They expect you to make them more important than your spouse, than your child, than your career—because in their mind, they *own you*. No matter where you go, where you work, where you live, they will always look at you and think, "They are *mine. They owe me everything.*" Because to them, they see themselves as so blindingly important that they are like the sun—without them, your little planet life would have nothing to orbit around. They believe that without them, you would be directionless, adrift, and waste away without their critical direction.

This is in part because of *enmeshment*. In a healthy relationship of any kind, two people exist as two separate, but potentially aligned entities. Enmeshment happens when people do not have a strong sense of boundaries, which means they have a hard time understanding where they stop and other people begin. To these types of poorly boundaried people, once you work for them, *you are a part of them*. To them, if you go off and join another organization, it's like telling them that their hand is no longer a part of their model. They believe they always have a claim on you, because in their mind, *they made you what you are*. They resent people who escape their orbit, and you should expect that they will sabotage future opportunities, provide poor references, or otherwise mess with your freedom and choices to try to force you into returning to them.

This means that when you leave an organization of someone like this, you need to be *extra careful.* When you negotiate mutual separation agreements or exit packages (which you should do every time you leave a role), you *must include* shadow blackballing kickers, or clauses that protect you from reputational harm by the organization. Otherwise, you may find that no matter how many interviews you do, you can't land a job in your industry again. This means putting in writing that your soon-to-be former bosses are prohibited from: 1) disparaging you to others, 2) interfering with other opportunities, and 3) engaging in crisis PR or reputational bot warfare, and that if they are caught doing those things, there are steep penalties that will make them think twice.

There is a unique piece of law in the US that works in your favor here. In 2023, the NLRB ruled that companies cannot require employees to sign nondisparagement clauses (only clauses that prohibit defamation). However, that law does not apply in reverse—you are allowed to request something that says something like, "[Overlord Entity], including but not limited to its officers, employees, agents, investors, contractors (including troll farms and bots), and affiliates, agrees that it shall not make any statements, whether written or oral, that are disparaging, derogatory, or harmful to the reputation of [you]. Further,

[Overlord Entity] shall not interfere, directly or indirectly, with any of [your] current or future business investment opportunities.

"In the event of a violation of this provision, [you] shall be entitled to seek injunctive relief and liquidated damages of [$X] per violation, in addition to any other remedies available at law or in equity."

The best example I have seen of this dynamic (in a way that I'm allowed to disclose) is in the popular show *Billions*. In it, the COO Wags is the prime example of a corporate "knight" who will go into battle at any cost for his feudal-lord-style CEO boss, Robert Axelrod. Importantly, you can see that most of Wags's identity comes from being in service to Axe, who he puts on a pedestal like a higher order of being. Later, you see Axe's protégé, Taylor, attempt to leave to start their own company. Axe resents that Taylor needs their own space and freedom to operate, and crushes/destroys Taylor's opportunities until they are forced to allow Axe to acquire their company back—completing the ownership cycle.

Have you ever been around someone who treated you like property? What was that like for you?

When They Make You See Red: How to Anchor

These types of leaders love to press buttons. If you tell them not to press a button in an elevator, they'll light up the entire board just to spite you.

So, when you're spending a lot of time with them, you need to be aware that they will be trying to get a rise out of you (or someone else near you), pretty much all the time.

Do not give them the satisfaction of a response.

Practice a bland, engaged expression that helps them know that if they metaphorically kick you, you will not yelp or cry.

But that's easier said than done. So, it's important to train yourself to raise your distress tolerance and emotionally regulate.

When they press your buttons, tell yourself, "I am

the sky, and my thoughts and feelings are the weather." Observe your emotions and thoughts without judgment. No matter how strong the storm, the sky's expanse contains it all. Let their attempts to unsettle you pass like momentary thunder.

If emotions are still running high, then engage acute distress tolerance skills.[1]

1. Remove yourself from the situation, so they can't press more of your buttons while you calm down. Turn your phone off if you need to. Go outside, take a walk, tell them you have to use the bathroom, whatever you need to do to create space.
2. Introduce a change in temperature—splash cold water on your face, put an ice cube in your hand, take a cold or hot shower, or go outside into the heat/cold without a coat.
3. Try some intense exercise. Strong body motions like jumping jacks or push-ups can help release the emotional energy.
4. Try paced breathing. Breathe in for a count of four, hold for a count of seven, then exhale for a count of eight.
5. Try progressive muscle relaxation. Bunch your arm muscles, squeezing as tight as you

---

1. Adapted from DBT distress tolerance skills (original philosophy written by Marsha Linehan).

can. Hold, then release. Then move to your legs, then your feet, then your forehead.

If you have to go back into the situation with them, then make sure you have a *buffer*. This should be either another person who they need to be on their best behavior for (e.g., to impress them), or someone else who is an alternate target. If you need to, organize a schedule in pairs where you rotate your team in and out to be on "leader duty." Make sure that you are not the only person who is taking the brunt of the button pushing.

Negotiating with Thieves: How to Rig the Game

I have negotiated with narcissists and psychopaths, when they controlled my world and I had no other choice. It's never fun. If possible, you should avoid being in situations where you have to negotiate with them at all.

If you can't avoid it, you have to go into the negotiation understanding that they do not care about you, and that they expect to shaft or jilt you. They will dangle hope, just for the fun of crushing you later. They see you as momentary entertainment that they enjoy toying with, just because they can.

So, expect them to negotiate in bad faith. They will not pay what they say they will; they will not do what they promise to. Assume that they will only give you 50 percent of what goes down on paper.

So, the key is to never let them know what it is that you really want or care about—and to plant false seeds that point them in the wrong direction. Pick a major piece of your "ask" to emphasize and make it sound like your key point, but expect to sacrifice it, along with something else. So, the best approach is usually to pick one big false flag that you "want," with two tack-ons, one of which you actually want.

Then, when they want to hurt you at the negotiating table, they'll be more likely to pull that major thing, and you can haggle over the remaining two, "compromising" on the thing you actually want.

Throughout the process, pretend that they are winning. Act sad, pretend to be mad as they take away pieces of what you "care" about—make them think they really got you. If you need to, threaten to resign. They will go away feeling self-satisfied, and they likely won't remember the thing you actually wanted.

For the one thing you do actually want, make the negotiation end on 200 percent of what you actually need. So, if you need $100,000 for your initiatives, start your ask at $400,000. Let them "beat you down" to $200,000, then expect them to actually follow through on paying half of that.

In business, your starting proposal to them might be:

- $1M for new employee restricted stock units
- $500K in learning stipends
- $400K in new software

Out of the gate, they'll try to cut the big thing first—the RSUs. Then, you would say, "Well, if I can't have that, give me the other two." Then, let them take away the learning stipends, and then negotiate down the software, ending with $200,000, twice as much as you need. To them, it looks like they reduced the ask by $1.7 million—but in reality, you just secured exactly what you need.

This may feel dishonest, but you have to remember that they are not honest, and that it is honorable to protect good people or initiatives. These types of leaders don't do what they say, and they're lying to you about what they're really committing to. This is one of the only ways to level the playing field.

This strategy applies universally to exploitative actors across business, government, and the social sector, and it aligns with known negotiation tactics used in high-stakes environments. Strategies like anchoring (providing the first number, then using it as an anchor), bracketing (providing false ranges), phantom concessions (pretending to give something meaningless), and red herrings (adding fake things one side does not care about) are commonly deployed in legal disputes, corporate dealmaking, and even intelligence operations. But most traditional negotiation training assumes ethical actors. When dealing with bad-faith players, you have to adapt, using their own tactics against them while keeping your integrity intact.

Don't Shop for Milk at the Hardware Store: Know What They're Good For

The next thing I want to explain is something colloquially called, "Don't shop for milk at the hardware store." It means that you will never be disappointed that a store doesn't have what you need if you know and remember what that store sells.

You could think of fear-based leaders as a *highly specific store*. They *do not* have the following on their shelves, and if you try to go into interactions seeking them, you will be very disappointed:

- Empathy
- Compassion
- Sympathy
- Understanding

- Validation
- Compromise
- Care
- Appreciation
- Logical strategy
- Agency
- Independence

So, do not expect your work to be appreciated. Do not expect flexible deadlines. Do not expect them to "get it" when you're sick and can't meet their needs. Do not expect them to ever listen to you speak about anything that is important to you, but not them. Do not expect them to meet you halfway. Do not expect them to remember your birthday, work anniversary, or life event.

You *can* expect their "store" to have the following in stock:

- Self-centeredness
- Brutality
- Destruction
- Capriciousness
- Spite
- Resentment
- Rage
- Grudges
- "My way or the highway"
- Cruelty
- Intolerance for dissent

- Impulsivity
- Emotional/power dynamic strategy
- Possessiveness
- Threats

If you go into every interaction with them with knowledge of what they are selling, you will never be surprised, disappointed, or taken aback. Once you internalize what kind of store you're in, you can also stop spending energy wishing it sold something different and start strategizing how to get what you need elsewhere.

It's easy to forget, but if time goes on and you still act like you're at a florist when you're at a granite quarry, then are sad when you don't see roses, but just a giant, empty hole, you need to adapt and adjust.

Let's practice.

Scenario 1: Tina is upset her boss did not seem to like her proposal. She isn't even sure he fully read it, and she spent two weeks on it. She complains to him that his reaction is unfair, and he yells at her for being a whiner.

Analysis: If her boss is a fear-based leader, then she is shopping at the wrong store—which should be clear to her by his outsized reaction. She should not expect any acknowledgment, praise, or kudos on any of her work. In this alternate reality, no news is good news.

Scenario 2: Avnish is trying to set up a strategic partnership with another company, but they won't meet him halfway on the ask. He pushes for weeks, and negotiations stall.

Analysis: If the CEO is a fear-based leader, they won't compromise at halfway. Avnish needs to make it feel like the other side is winning to get what he wants.

Scenario 3: Erica only ever brings her boss problems when they are attached to a solution—and a solution that is framed to make the boss look especially good.

Analysis: Erica is remembering what type of store she is at, and is framing things in a way that serves self-serving people. Good work, Erica!

Part of what makes all of this difficult is the wishful thinking involved. It's *hard* to remember what store you're at, because you likely don't *want* to be at that store. But do not let that trip you up. You need to see clearly, to protect what's most important to you. Once you *do* see, then you're operating in a more empowered way—you are free from the disappointment of not being at the store you expected, and have the mental space to shop what is actually available for purchase.

A Lesson in Discernment: Actions vs. Words

People get strung along by the promises of egocentric leaders because they want to believe what they say. But if you track their actions versus their words, you can get a clearer view of what they're *actually* saying, and whether they'll deliver on their promises.

Recently, I went through the process of retaining five separate types of lawyers. One potential counsel said great things on calls, like, "I want this case. I'd love to work with you. I'll send you a retainer." But after the first time she said that, a week went by, and she didn't send a retainer. I met with her again. She said the same thing, while expressing some reservations about demand value—but ten days later, no retainer. I left messages with her office to no avail.

Her *words* were telling me that she was enthusiastic. But her *actions* were telling me not so much. In fact, her actions and tone told me over that period that 1) she was so inconsiderate that she wasted three weeks of my statute of limitations on a very time-sensitive case, 2) she wanted to put me in my place as the client and see if I'd "fall in line" and chase her, and 3) if she didn't feel like talking to me *during* the case, she would probably ghost me then too.

This is why it's important to listen with both your ears and your eyes. Your ears are for what someone directly tells you. Your eyes will tell you the true story—by tracking their actions.

Silicon Valley is much like this. So much so that in my music album, I wrote a song about it. It goes like this:

California Coffee Chat

[verse 1]
It's been too long
We should meet for lunch
Let's get together
We'll make it happen

[verse 2]
You're just super
I love talking to you
Let's find the truth together
I just want the answers

[verse 3]
Oh, by the way
Won't you look at my pitch?
Can you cofound?
I need some advice

[chorus]
This has been so nice
Let's do this again
We should stay in touch
You're such a doll

[bridge]
Just to translate:
I hate your guts
If I never saw you again
It'd make my day
I will talk to you
If you have something I need
I want to succeed
You are an obstacle
Won't you just sign
My NDA
It's for the best

[chorus]
This has been so nice
Let's do this again

We should stay in touch
You're such a doll

The *surface message* is that someone *loves* this person they ran into. But underneath the surface and in their actions (blowing them off, not scheduling additional coffees, not making intros they promised to make, etc.), they *hate* this person, and only interact with them to extract value when they absolutely have to.

The reason people *say* nice things is because 50 percent of the people they interact with actually believe the niceties—partly, because they want them to be true—and that misdirection, or mismatching actions and words, often keeps people from setting up opposition to their aims.

Don't let yourself be easily misdirected. Some people lie because they're protecting themselves from consequences, inconvenience, discomfort, or conflict. Others lie because they're protecting themselves from their own awareness (they're deceiving themselves and, by extension, you). Either way, misdirection is a sign of fear, and if you see a mismatch between words and actions often, take note—and stop believing what that person tells you with their words. On the other hand, you can *always* believe their actions.

Another time I ran into this was with a manager at work, who was extremely politically savvy, and very charismatic. She would say things like, "I just want to make sure you're set up for success. I want to make sure that you're cared for." And then she would go ahead and reply to none of my emails, refuse to comment on my work or provide performance feedback, cancel half my one-on-ones, set me up to fail in meetings, refuse to do my reviews, and refuse to help with issues with other departments. I *wanted* to believe she cared but was just a bad manager. But because I *knew* that she was extremely capable and politically savvy, I knew that *actually* she had been told I was political kryptonite, and given instructions to make sure there was a basis for negative feedback, so that I could be pushed out of the company.

It would have been tempting to just put my head in the sand—and go "la la la la, I can't hear you, reality"—but instead, I started taking my own actions to leave the firm on my own terms.

This week, pick one person in your life and write down some of the things they tell you. Then, write down the ten major things you see them do throughout the week. Do they match?

Remember that discernment isn't cynicism—it's just recognizing the truth of where you are, so you can decide where you want to go.

You're Just Imagining Things: How to Resist Brainwashing

There is another type of misdirection that I would be remiss not to cover, and that is brainwashing. Like the previous topic, this is something I have written music about ... because it is, essentially, writing a new soundtrack over your own track of self-trust and self-belief. It's insidious, and can eat at you from the inside.

Here's how it works:

First, the leader gauges your level of self-trust. Weaker, less confident people are easier targets. Naive people are easier targets.

Then, they try to *interfere with the stage at which your perceptions become fact in your mind*. The best way to control someone is by making them *only believe in what you say, not what they see*. It is at its core a way to take someone from true reality, pluck them out, and drop them into the leader's *distorted reality*.

That sounds hard to do. It's not—not at all.

It often sounds like this:

- "You're so sensitive."
- "You're just imagining things."
- "That's not really what happened."
- "That's not what I saw."
- "This is all in your head."
- "No one would believe you anyway."
- "You're not really unhappy. You're just dreaming."
- "You're not really sick. It doesn't really hurt. You're just delicate."
- "You aren't smart enough to see the truth."
- "The only person you can trust is me."
- "Without me, you would be totally lost."
- "You can't do anything without me."
- "You're incapable."

The fear-based leader will test a rotating variety of these phrases on you, studying to see which actually confuses you and makes you stop fighting back against them. Then they will double down and repeat, repeat, repeat it day in and day out until doubt creeps into your mind. Maybe I *don't* know what I'm talking about. Maybe I *am* helpless. And that's when they've got you—if you stop believing what you're seeing, they can tell you anything is true, and you'll go along with it. Voilà, they can get away with anything.

In most cases, you do not want to stand up overtly to a fear-based leader because they'll see it as defiance and label you as an enemy. The exception is gaslighting. It is *extremely important* that as soon as they start testing this on you, you send a signal that this is not going to work on you and you're nipping it in the bud.

Here's what that sounds like:

- "That's not true, you don't know anything at all, you're just a mindless worm." → "I know what is real and true."
- "I'm not embezzling, you just don't understand accounting." → "I am qualified and accurate."
- "You're just imagining that firing half our staff will hurt our customers." → "No, I am not."

Don't get baited into an argument—just reply firmly and simply, in a way that says, "Uh-uh, this is not going to work on me." Otherwise, they'll essentially start brainwashing you, and you won't be able to stop it. When you hear something enough, and it becomes familiar, it starts to feel true even when it's not.

Control Over Connection: How to Bend, Not Snap

People who aren't brave enough to bare their souls in the vulnerability to connect choose control instead. It is relatedness, not relationship, with a buffered distance that feels safer—distance between the people on and beneath the pedestal.

People who try to feed their souls with control end up chasing emptiness, going after power for power's sake, unaware that it is taking a step down to be equal that will truly nourish them.

People who are obsessed with control loathe those who they perceive as undisciplined or emotional—and they like to toy with their prey.

It can be hard to believe that there are people who allow others to dangle, or genuflect, just to test the limits of how hard and deeply someone can control them.

But their disdain renders others who lack control around them subhuman in their eyes.

Do not be surprised if you see these types of leaders pushing those around them further and further, just for the satisfaction of watching them snap.

It's a lot like fishing—baiting others to see how long it takes them to have their emotions rise and rule them instead of cold analysis and logic. For the fear-based leader, it's a reassuring confirmation of their own superiority.

It is one of the few things that doesn't bore them, because it provides a rush of heady ego when their ability to crush is validated. You might bend a pen cap until it breaks, or pick at a mosquito bite. Instead, they pick at people for the pleasure of opening scabs, and even better if an infection takes hold. In their minds, this is part of natural selection—they're just accelerating survival of the fittest.

I have watched psychopaths do this until all the people around them are broken, unable to trust, form healthy relationships, or like themselves. They are then content to rule over their court of broken toys.

If they try this with you, don't give them the satisfaction of seeing you bend or snap. Several people have tried this on me from the time I was a young child. In one notable case, a manager told me that she was deliberately trying to make me suffer more than her other reports, that she wished she could make me suffer more in silence, and that while it normally took her two months to break her reports down, she was confounded that she'd hazed me for ten months with absolutely no luck.

She never did break me. And I went on to successfully start my own business, start advocacy projects, write a music album and comedy special, and write this book, while she is still exactly where I left her—hating her life, her kids, her responsibilities, and her job.

When you are facing headwinds and players like this, imagine that you are reeds in a marsh, dancing in the wind. When the wind blows, you move with it, always springing right back to where you started when it relents. You are flexible. You are rooted. And the wind may brush you, but you know how to dance.

Fewer and Better: How to Prioritize

When a lot is at stake, it can be easy to want to hold on to everything at once. You cannot protect it all. So you need to prioritize.

Here are some dimensions you can choose to prioritize:

- Breadth of impact (affecting a million users, patients, etc.)
- Depth of impact (saving each user a ton of time/money/suffering)
- Personal importance (I want to help cancer patients because my mom died of cancer)
- Societal importance (collectively, society needs companies that help children)

- Hard ROI (we will earn 80% margin on these products)
- Minimization of suffering (200K patients will not have HIV)
- Lives saved (100 people in our clinical trials will have a new lease on life)

Whatever you do choose, keep your focus on protecting no more than a few precious things. With the startup CEOs I coach, I have a rule of thumb called, "No more product lines than investors on your cap table." It's a way of saying, "Do a few things well, rather than a bunch of things halfway. Later on, the more resources you have, the more you can do."

Fear-based leaders will give you some degree of latitude if you present as a loyal lackey. But, not a totally open, wide field of latitude. You can be the hard-ass direct report with an eccentric soft spot for a certain program—but you cannot be someone who is totally made up of soft spots and still be accepted. So, choose wisely, and then hold on tight.

Another way to think about this is in a system of *points.* Imagine that every initiative you do in favor of the fear-based leader gives you 10 points. Now, every initiative that's your pet initiative—something important to you, but not to them—is –40 points.

It doesn't matter how many pet initiatives you have, so long as your balance stays above zero. But if you want to have maximum impact and maximum latitude, drive up ten of the fear-based leader's initiatives, so you're valuable enough to have plenty of points in the bank when there's something you need to draw down for.

Familiarity ≠ Safety: Don't Get Comfortable

As I spoke to a friend today, I said something that may sound counterintuitive to you as a reader: When things start to feel familiar to me, something is about to go majorly wrong. This is because the environments that my personal algorithm was originally tuned to as a child were deeply wrong—full of depravity, cruelty, and corruption to a degree that it would be hard for many of you to imagine.

This is the *opposite* of how most people work—and this is something you have to keep in mind when you stay in the environment surrounding a fear-based leader.

You *cannot let your guard down.* You *cannot settle in.*

Do everything you can to maintain the degree of sensitivity you had when you joined the environment. Watch movies where the good guy wins. Go to your faith community. Spend time with children, and with friends who are completely unrelated to this leadership environment. Do everything you can to remind yourself that *those* are what is normal—not where you're spending your days. *Don't let the fear-based leader skew your algorithm.*

Because it's only natural that over time, you want to relax. But if you do relax, what is *normal* to you is going to shift. And over time, what is *familiar* starts to feel like what is *safe*—but the *danger is still there.* Just because the people you see and interact with in the halls know your name, doesn't mean they care about you. They'd likely stab you in the back just as soon as you turn around, so they can climb the ladder to be where you are.

I have run into this trap myself before. On my very first day in my new office in private equity, a senior colleague was pleasant to my face, then threw me under the bus with a scathing review to my new manager. That woke me up—I wasn't in Kansas (or in my case, Ohio), anymore. But over the next several years, the zero-sum, cutthroat behavior became so commonplace that it no longer shocked me. It was business as usual, and barely registered as part of my day. Because I was *used to it*, it wasn't until I gave a timeline of my entire time working at that company to an employment lawyer that I realized that the company had been systemically mistreating me, undercompensating me, and aggressively torpedoing my career in an incredibly significant cumulative pattern.

This is where it can get confusing: Is the devil you know better than the devil you don't know? In all truth, that depends—you should stay if there is something worth protecting that won't destroy your health or well-being. But you should go if there's nothing you can save, if the environment is eating your soul, or if you have much better things to do. Only ever stay in an environment if *you are taking more from it than it is from you.*

You may be a part of an organization, but that organization is also part of you—part of your story, your learning, your development. It extracts value from you, and you need to actively extract from it, be that experience, connections, credentialing, learning, money, or clout.

In my case, my work at that firm gave me incredible street cred in my industry, taught me things I use in my coaching practice, honed my strategic skill set, and gave me good health insurance for years of health challenges. But the company also caused me to have severe health issues, and it was an aggressive, abrasive place that gave me little pleasure to be in. So once I got what I needed, I left.

I tell people the same thing when they ask me about joining consulting firms like my first employer. In consulting, *you* are the company's product, so the company pours all its R&D into your brain. It wants you to learn and grow as fast as possible to become an optimal tool—and in the process of those eighty-hour weeks, your capacity expands, your problem-solving ability grows, and you become well versed in many industries and functions. But there's a saying: The top 25 percent leave the firm after a few years because they have better things to do, the bottom 25 percent can't hack it, and it's the middle who stays—because most talented, non-risk-averse people are able to make the call of when they've taken as much as they can from the firm and it's time to leave the training ground to test themselves on the real world.

It's up to you to make sure that you don't let unhealthy behaviors become "normal"—and also up to you to decide whether something is worth your while. Every year, I recommend writing up what matters most to you in a job, then checking how well your current role measures up. If it doesn't, that's okay—there is nothing wrong with something ending. As important as it is to protect users, consumers, patients, etc., you can't do any of that if you aren't able to be energized or aren't well enough to do your part.

No One Can Cage You Without Your Consent: Find the Space

There have been times in life when my world felt like it was shrinking. When I realized I couldn't travel places that didn't have a developed-world hospital within an hour away. When I was unable to be vaccinated due to infections and had to stop going to conferences for a while. When I encountered people in business and in life who tried to put walls around me—like when I was about to leave my last company, and they started killing all my opportunities for advancement.

My specialty is creative problem solving in the face of hard constraints—I love to help clients with that—but when I have to apply that tool kit to my personal life, I sometimes feel sad. I never thought I'd need that toolbox again.

It's at those times that a wise advisor told me to look for the spaces, not the fence. Here's what I mean: Imagine a white picket fence around a green field. Most people look at it and they see the slats in the fence, the gates, the locks. But if you look at the spaces in between the slats instead, instead of seeing a *barrier*, you see *opportunities*.

This is where we get to an old saying, one said to be from Eleanor Roosevelt: "No one can make you feel inferior without your consent." This is true, but it can feel abstract. Here is *why* that's true. Fear-based leaders exist because they are on a pedestal—but the thing is, people can only be on a pedestal if other people put them there. For them to be *above* others, others have to kneel before them, or elevate them by kowtowing. If you don't do those things, you just have a greatly self-important person on flat ground next to you.

When people like this try to create constraints around me, I laugh at them. They see themselves as giants casting a huge shadow, big and scary, and I see them like tiny tin soldiers that I could knock over with a Nerf gun.

I would amend Eleanor's statement to say, "No one can cage me without my consent." Why? Because *I am like water*. Build a fence around me, and I will flow out like I was never there to begin with, laughing the whole time about how someone puny and insecure ever thought they could contain someone as whole, strong, vibrant, and principled as me.

When you change the way you look at things, the things you look at change. See the spaces between the slats. For me, that meant saying, "Okay, there are places I can't travel anymore . . . There are things that I cannot do due to health reasons. What are ways that I can increase my types of new experiences, without going anywhere?" Well, by writing comedy, music, and books like this one, I open the door to connect with thousands of people that I would never otherwise meet—just like when I travel. I am exposed to new viewpoints, and like-minded people find me because I'm putting myself out in the world, even without going anywhere. I avidly check out new restaurants that bring different cuisines to my city, and visit neighborhoods where I don't speak the language, to soak up different cultures . . . and my cup is full. Even if I had to stay within driving distance of home the entire rest of my life, I don't think I'd ever run out of things to do.

Explore the space left in your life, despite the constraints you may be under. It may be roomier than you think.

You Have Permission to Move: Get Unstuck

A lot of people will not be able to hear and process what I write, because they are determined to stay stuck in bad situations. Their consciousness sees *value* in the stuckness, so it doesn't allow disruptive information to make it through. They could read this entire book and take nothing from it.

This is not because they are bad people—even though this applies to about 80 percent of the people I meet—it's more like someone has told them that it's very important that they stay very still and not move, so they forget they can move at all.

My goal is to help even those people start to see a way out—and to keep you from falling for that in the first place.

There are many paralyzing forces in our society, and

fear-based leaders will use them to try to make you think that you're stuck. These are weapons like shame, social conformity, fear, telling people to stay small, and rewarding obedience over insight.

This sounds like:

- Shame: "You're such a bad person, I can't believe you did XYZ."
- Social conformity: "Your sweater is so weird, did your mom pick that out for you?"
- Fear: "Get off my bed right now or you'll be sorry."
- Stay small: "I don't know why you want to move to the big city, anyway. Don't you love us?"
- Rewarding obedience: "I know I can always count on you to do exactly what you're told."

Sometimes, people realize they can get attention when bad things happen to them—like being sick, or having a terrible boss—and the sympathetic outrage and attention feeds them and their ego, so that it becomes something that makes them feel alive. So, they become addicted to the drama. It's like having a bad boyfriend—the push and pull of a codependent relationship becomes a tasty, junk food type of chaos.

This may not be you. But it will certainly be many people around you. In several cases, I have had friends be very sick, and I recognized immediately what illness they had from the hundreds of hours I've spent with medical specialists. But when I mentioned gently what it could be, and offered a referral for a professional who could provide confirmation, they said, "No thanks." They'd rather be sick—and they stay sick, often with debilitating symptoms. So because I cannot say this to them, I want to say to you very clearly: When it feels like you are stuck . . .

You are allowed to move. You will find ways to feel alive that are not drama cycles. But to do that, you need the courage to try new things, and stop repeating the same mistakes over and over again.

I give you permission to try. I give you permission to fail. I give you permission to be who you have always wanted to be. If not now, when?

False Generosity: Find the String

Something that often initially confuses people about fear-based leaders is that they don't seem "all bad." They have moments where they seem, well, quite good.

Usually, those are moments of generosity.

This is where it's important not to project your own moral compass on someone else. Likely when you give a gift, you give it because it brings you joy, or you want to bring someone else joy.

Fear-based leaders are not like that. If they enjoy gift giving, it's for one of a few common reasons: 1) It brings them adulation, which feeds their ego, or 2) it gives them a hold (control) over the recipient.

What you don't realize when the gift is offered is that every "gift" from a transactional person is not a gift, it is a *string*. Putting a deposit down in your account is like an IOU for a future favor—one that will always be repaid later. So, it pays for the leader to be generous, because it means they are always *owed*, and that in most situations, they will have the *upper hand*.

They will often tell you directly that something is "out of the goodness of their heart" or "no strings attached" or "it makes me happy to see you happy." All of that is a lie. Don't believe them. They'll make it clear either up front, or months later, what they actually wanted and expect.

So, beware. It's like signing a contract where you can't read the terms. It's wishful thinking to see their giving as proof of them being a good person—but think of the generous acts not as a form of altruism, but an investment in your future obedience or loyalty. Pat pat, give the dog a bone.

This means that you have a few options: 1) You can politely deflect offers of generosity ("Oh, I couldn't possibly; please find someone more deserving"; "That's far too much, I really can't; thank you for thinking of me"), 2) you can take what they give, and void the contract by refusing to provide what they want later, or 3) you can play along, angling for the favors you want and paying them back in turn.

They will not be dissuaded easily if you deflect—so if that fails, move to number three, both pushing with subtle hints of what you want ("I just don't know what to do; I can't figure out how to make this contract aboveboard; if only there was someone who could help with that"— this plays into them thinking everyone around them is incapable, and gives them a chance to be a savior), and doing *them* unexpected favors so they owe you (this keeps them off balance).

The favors might seem innocuous—they might offer to get a relative an internship, help you get out of a parking ticket, or give you tickets to see *Hamilton*. The thing is, these are *not* legal contracts. Gifts freely given under the law cannot have secret terms. So my favorite way to deal with this is number two, to *pretend* to be obedient, then pretend like I'm an idiot who didn't understand that there was a string. "Oh, you'd like me to listen to you monologue every week because you gave me that hire I asked for? I couldn't possibly do that; everyone knows that I am nothing but devoted to my team, and they desperately need me right now. But Joe on my team is always asking to learn from you; he'll set up some time so he can benefit from your wealth of expertise" (void the contract and stroke their ego).

In a world full of strings, your best defense is remembering who you are, and what you actually owe.

Finding Good Pockets in Bad Places: Learn to Diligence

Even in fear-based organizations, there are often small pockets of health and safety. I call these *good pockets*—and learning how to find them will help you survive as long as possible (maybe even thrive).

Most organizations have what you could think of as negative and positive flywheels. A negative section of the company might have bad leadership, mean managers, and incompetent employees. People who enter this swirling vortex find their career trending downward. No mentorship, no sponsorship, always-missed project milestones . . . It's a sinkhole. A positive section of the company has good enough leaders, good enough managers, and good enough direct reports. There's less fear, and more teamwork. People there find themselves growing, being given more opportunities, and feeling good about their work.

So how do you find the good pockets?

In venture capital, we call it *diligencing*. It means deeply studying your target so that you understand what you're getting into before you commit.

This might mean finding a section of your company where eight of ten team members tell you they love their manager when you invite them for a coffee chat. It's important to ask questions obliquely, because people feel bad about saying negative things point blank.

If you want to know if you'll be run ragged, you can ask specific but indirect questions (e.g., "What has your manager done to invest in your development since you joined?") to see if they think intentionally about this at all. Or, "What are the times of your usual working sessions?" to see if they're working nights. The key is to be *specific* and avoid people becoming *defensive*.

After you start asking the questions, you have to decide whether they are telling the truth. A good rule of thumb is that negative feedback is true 80 percent of the time—but positive references are white lies 50 percent of the time, or more.

Why? Teams that are stuck in negative cycles are desperate for reasonable people to join them—so they're not suffering alone—and they are often short staffed, meaning they need bodies to alleviate the pressure on them.

And, for especially negative people, the people around them are afraid that the negative diligence will get back to the bad actor.

A very good hint of whether someone is lying is whether their positive notes are generic or specific.

If a leader is actually very good, people will have endless examples of what, specifically, that person has done to help their cause or career. They will be able to list what they learned, what they love about the person, and why they want to stay working there. If, on the other hand, you hear "Jenny is great!" "Steve is the best!" "Akash is a good manager"—that does not pass the sniff test.

When diligencing, remember people have many different facets. Every time there's a power dynamic difference, people show a different face. The way Charlie treats a male manager outside of his org at basketball may be very different than how he treats a junior female report on his team at work. So if you're someone who's going to be reporting to him, find the closest person to you possible (make it apples to apples).

This is where how you ask questions will make a difference. You could ask your potential colleagues, "How long do his direct reports tend to stay with him? Can I speak with someone who recently left his team?" If they obfuscate, *it's not a fit*.

Power Corrupts: How to Stay Whole

A lot of people have heard the phrase "absolute power corrupts absolutely."[1]

This is not just an axiom—it's supported by science. Several years ago there was an article in *The Atlantic* in which the reporter covered the phenomenon in which power literally corroded the centers in people's brains responsible for empathy.[2]

The more money, power, or status someone has, the less they tend to follow the rules—both because they feel like they're above them, and because the cost of breaking them is lower. If you make minimum wage, a $500

---

1. From Lord Acton.
2. From Jerry Useem, "Power Causes Brain Damage," *The Atlantic*, July/August 2017, https://www.theatlantic.com/magazine/archive/2017/07/power-causes-brain-damage/528711/.

speeding ticket can cause you to not eat for a month. If you have a lot of money, that might be the cost of giving up one nice dinner out with your family—no big deal, essentially.

So, it's important that you internalize that, from my experience, an estimated 70-plus percent of leaders are self-interested and morally bankrupt—not because they started out that way, but because of what their power has done to them.

It's also important that you make sure you don't let this happen to you.

The best way to avoid being corrupted by power is to not chase it or cling to it. If you have to have it, be someone who has it not because you want it, but because there is either no one else to do it, or other people have chosen you over all other options.

When you are in positions of power, pay attention to both your successes and mistakes. I know that if I haven't made five mistakes by lunchtime, I'm either lacking self-awareness, or not challenging myself enough. Constantly put yourself in situations where you're the least knowledgeable person in the room, so that you constantly grow. Remind yourself how little any of us truly knows.

Don't be afraid of admitting when you don't know something. Do that often. Always apologize and take accountability when you make a mistake. When people do things that you don't expect, get curious, and put yourself in their shoes, and seek to understand, not dominate.

Put your values up on the wall in your office, and

remind yourself what your north star is. Once a month, ask yourself how well you're living your values.

Remind yourself that everyone else is no more, and no less, than your equal. And when you can, try to do small kindnesses.

Make your employees or group members actively practice dissent. Reward people who admit their mistakes, as opportunities to learn and grow. Make sure that everyone always feels safe enough to come to you with anything that doesn't feel right, so that things don't get swept under the rug. Listen more than you talk. Ask more questions than you make statements. As a manager, only do the things that only you can do, and the rest of the time, trust your people and get out of their way.

If you do these things, you will not become a fear-based leader, because the people around you will not put you on a pedestal, but see you as a peer. Even if you don't hold formal power yet, you hold influence. Every time you choose curiosity over control, values over vanity, integrity over ego, you build a foundation strong enough to resist corruption.

The Sword of Perception: How to See Through Halos

Scientists have identified different types of halo effects.[1] For example, very beautiful people are assumed to be more moral, or more intelligent. Very tall people are more often looked to as leaders. But there are many, many more types of halos than just those related to physical appearance, and no one that I know of has written about how halos exist on a *spectrum*.

It's important that you understand how these work, so that you're not blinded by the social trappings of fear-based leaders. You need to be able to see past their halos to correctly identify them for what they are. So, I'm going to explain my theory about this, to essentially give you some sunglasses to cut down on the glare.

---

1. Term originally coined by Thorndike.

Here are some common types of halos:

- Someone is wealthy, so they must be competent.
- Someone is a leader, so they must have earned it.
- Someone is beautiful, so they must be kind.
- Someone is cute, so they must be innocent, and need protection.
- Someone has a big lexicon, and always knows about a cool new thing, so they must be cultured.
- Someone has an emotionally compelling narrative, so everything else they do must also be meaningful or justified.
- Someone seems gentle, so they must be weak.
- Someone acts kind, so they must be morally good.
- Someone is loved/trusted by a vulnerable child/elder/pet, so they must be safe.
- Someone has suffered, so they must be saintly.
- Someone is confident, so they must be right.
- Someone is loud, so I should listen to them more than others.

You could think of all of these "halos" as shortcuts for your brain—ways to make interpreting the world and people around you easier, so your brain has to do less processing. However, almost all of them are logical fallacies—the if-then statements break down under scrutiny. If you spend time around a fear-based leader and let these types of narratives dominate, you will be sticking your head in the sand and underestimating the danger and pathology around you.

Most literature about halos talks solely about positive effects. However, you should think of halos as if they exist at one end of a spectrum—the positive end, that adds points to someone's overall image. There is also a *negative end*, on the opposite side of the spectrum. I call these *shadows*, because the assumptions people make about others who have these traits lead to pejorative stigmas.

Together, they form a double-edged sword. The halo side of that sword can tap your shoulders, to essentially bestow a status of modern knighthood. The shadow side can carve your reputation into shreds. Here are some examples of shadows:

- If someone is fat, they are lazy.
- If someone is ugly, they are less likable.
- If someone lacks confidence, they aren't smart or capable.

And so on. Every halo has an inverse that's a shadow. If wealth gives you positive perception points, poverty gives you negative. If being tall gives you leadership status, being short takes leadership odds away. And so on.

The two best examples that I know of, that may paint

a clearer picture of how halos and shadows work for you, are about dogs and kids.

I am a warm, friendly person; I like talking to my neighbors, and am always friendly when they speak with me. However, until I adopted my service dog, Annie, they rarely spoke to me; in fact, they mostly ignored me. Within weeks of adopting her, their entire demeanor towards me changed. All of a sudden, stone-faced tech workers were smiling, asking me questions, chatting in the elevator, and stopping me on the street to say hello. I realized that my association with Annie was deeply humanizing. Their subconscious was saying things like, "Kate must be kind, because Annie trusts her. She must be responsible, because Annie is so happy and calm. She must be approachable, because Annie is so friendly. She must be trustworthy, because Annie is so relaxed around her." It became a legitimate endorsement of my character.

The *opposite* often happens with people with kids. Many parents (especially those who are enmeshed or codependent) struggle to see their kids as independent figures, who are not extensions of their own person. However, this is also partly due to how society treats them. Society judges parents, especially mothers, scathingly. There, the shadow effect goes, "The kids are running wild; the parent is lazy and not paying enough attention. The kids were rude and didn't say thank you; their parents are not teaching them moral character. That toddler is having a tantrum; the parent is a moron who can't control their child."

The halo blinds people to flaws so that those around the person cannot see their faults. The shadows darken someone's image, so that the people around them cannot see their strengths.

In the middle is the mean, where perceptions are more measured and accurate—but most people don't exist there. This is not a bell curve; people in power tend to cluster towards either end of the spectrum. If you exist with a halo, life is easier for you in almost every way. If you are shrouded in shadows, you have to claw your way to success because you're starting with a negative balance, and have to clear the deficit in perception before the people around show you respect and consideration. The same behavior that is forgiven under a halo effect is condemned and punitive under a shadow. A very handsome new sales hire who bullshits his way through a meeting is seen as bold; an ugly, fat one is punished for "going off script." The mean is not so much a place where you can stay, but a temporary place where you teeter until you reveal something about yourself that pushes you one way or the other.

Fear-based leaders are very aware of halos and shadows. And, because they're aware, and most of the world isn't, they maneuver and manipulate within them. They craft personas to hide and obscure their intentions—and you absolutely need to be able to see through the moral camouflage. Some common ways they mislead others:

- Flaunting wealth and generosity (e.g., hosting a company party at their huge house)

- Being strongly affiliated with religion (hiding behind being "God fearing" or devout to hide their true allegiance, to themselves)
- Surrounding themselves with people who have shadows, so they look like they have a comparative halo
- Telling stories that emphasize the degree of power they are able to exert over others, to seem deeply in control
- Sowing favors with media to ensure favorable coverage—or buying media companies to program the coverage
- Using NDAs to silence the people around them who see the bad behavior

They are not the only ones who can influence the halos and shadows surrounding them. The easiest ones to take on are **appearance halos, association halos,** and **proximity halos.** Invest in a very good, modern haircut; pay attention to style trends and make sure that your clothes fit and flatter. Associate yourself with strong brands that provide lift through association: working for credible companies, going to the best schools you can get into and afford, seeking mentors you genuinely admire. And try to make sure that you are always the least smart person in the room: Surround yourself with the most kind, brilliant, and good people you can possibly find, and they will lift you with them.

Misleading Marketing: How Not to Fall for It

Similar to gaslighting—where you're told one thing is true, but it's actually the opposite—fear-based leaders will often try to *sell* you on things that are harmful for you. They might make people compete for the opportunity to do something that is unappealing or dangerous, or present something as a reward that is actually a punishment. This is misleading marketing.

Here's an example. What if I told you, tomorrow I'm going to take you away from everything you love—your family, friends, restaurants, hobbies—and starve you for a month. You'll be stranded outdoors and have to sleep on the ground in the rain in areas where there are snakes and rodents, and you'll be with complete strangers who may or may not be friendly or stable. There will be no laundry, no bathrooms, no showers, no camping supplies. You'll have no privacy, and in fact all your worst moments will be recorded and shown to everyone you've ever known. And every other day, I'll make you run through a human maze to test how fast and strong you are. If you don't perform well, I'll let you go back home.

This sounds like forced homelessness with public shaming, right? No one would want that. Everyone would intentionally fail the maze so they'd be allowed to go home, right?

No—actually, the opposite. This is a description of what I consider to be the longest running test of corporate marketing efficacy on a population. Every year, Jeff Probst tells people that the opportunity is scarce and only the very best candidates will be chosen to go on *Survivor*, and people apply by the thousands for a 5 percent chance at a post-tax $600,000.

Never mind that contestants claim publicly afterwards that the media attention ruined their life—and that the paranoia and sheer scarcity affect their ability to form normal relationships for years. Never mind that contestants have gotten so extremely sick from parasites in the food and water that they've been ill for years after filming. Never mind that $600,000 is not enough to retire on, send three kids to private college, or buy a mansion.

Both contestants and audiences lap up the narrative that watching other humans break down and suffer is not sadistic, but entertainment—because that's what the commercials tell them it is. No comments are made about the voyeurism of a developed-world country letting its globally wealthy citizens pretend to be an impoverished Indigenous tribe complete with names like "Tuvalu" or "Tiki," testing out destitution for a month as a thrill when many people around the world live that way with no choice.

In the last three seasons, some of the contestants have woken up from their marketing-lulled stupor and quit the show midseason because they realized how deeply unpleasant, gritty, and unsafe the situations are. Jeff always acts like they're aberrations for not drinking the Kool-Aid—a casting failure in the psych screen—rather than a sign that the world is getting more boundaried, more healthy, and less willing to tolerate abuse, even though they're told the abuse is an exciting opportunity for them.

Don't fall for messaging like *Survivor* contestants do. Ask yourself questions: What would I say about all this if it was without any hype? Told to me by someone with zero charisma? In a situation where my friends weren't raving about it? How would I react if someone offered this to me in a dark alley, rather than on primetime TV?

Cultivate your inner voice—because it's what will help you see through the spin and momentum to what is actually true. Make a small promise to yourself every day, and keep it—I will walk for five minutes, I will journal before bed, I will eat my vegetables—to strengthen your self-trust muscle so that when everything around you is telling you not to believe your senses, your inner voice and truth will win out, instead.

If You Give a Mouse a Cookie:[1] How to Avoid Slippery Slopes

There is a very cute children's book, in which a little mouse asks for a cookie. But then, when he's given the cookie, he asks for a glass of milk. Once he has the glass of milk, he wants something else.

This is the nature of a fear-based leader.

They're never satisfied. They are like a giant, empty black hole—or a very, very hungry cookie monster—and once you give them a cookie, there's a chance they might devour the plate, and then your arm, and then you.

People often go into negotiations with them, thinking that if they just capitulate, they can move on with their life. But giving them one thing is just the gateway to

---

1. Reference to the book by Laura Numeroff.

giving them something else. It creates a tie between you that they will pull harder and harder on.

Their goal is complete subjugation—that they get everything good that you might have, just so that you can't have it. Not because they don't have enough, or because they really enjoy the things they take—but because they enjoy the feeling of them having something that you want.

So when given a choice, do not feed the monster. Do not think that giving in to their first ask will keep them from having a second ask. It will in fact guarantee that the second ask is larger.

It can feel completely damned if you do, damned if you don't. Don't give them something, and they'll try to stomp you. Give them something, and they'll try to devour you.

In my opinion, it's better to give them nothing, than to give them something. Because it's in that version of the world that you get to keep your dignity, and your integrity.

If you must give them something, make it something very unsatisfying. If the person hates books, give them your book collection. If they like shiny things, give them something ordinary and dull. *Make them think you're so boring, you have nothing good to give.*

People like this can strike at very unexpected times, so try not to show them anything good you have at all.

I once showed a fear-based leader a gift I was planning to give someone—and he immediately pouted, "Where's *my* present?" even though I had several presents ready for him. He didn't care that I had five presents for him—he wanted *exactly what I was giving to someone else*, and demanded that I add a sixth present for him to make up for the fact that I had not planned to give him that exact thing, too. Another time, I had to borrow something from a fear-based leader on short notice, to avoid a social faux pas at a meeting. The next day, I brought him something nicer and more expensive in return, as a thank-you. But, it wasn't enough—later that day, he saw something I had bought for myself and he claimed it. He stole it from me as "repayment" for the item I had to borrow—and years later, he posts photos of it multiple times a year, rubbing it in that he has something of mine.

Sounds petty, right? *They are petty.* Expect nothing less. And when you have good things, keep it to yourself.

Manufactured Chaos: It's Intentional

Something that I see all the time with the startup founders I coach are complaints from their teams about *chaos*: "My team says I need to stop changing my mind all the time, but I'm trying to adapt to the market"; "All startups have ups and downs; why doesn't my team get it?"

What these founders sometimes don't see is how their sense of what is *familiar* is impacting the environments they create around them.

Most fear-based leaders (and many strong startup founders) grow up in chaotic environments with unpredictable people. They are not able to form enduring, stable relationships with parental figures, because the parents are either unavailable (like many immigrant parents), not well (like many who struggle with mental health or addiction), or prize external image over wellbeing (like families who care about their societal reputation over internal connection).

What this means is that these leaders often then replicate instability in the environments they create, because to them, *instability feels safe*. It's what they know. And a lot of them are trying desperately to prove that *they are enough* to the people who found them lacking when they were young—by making a lot of money, getting the highest job title, or having a fancy, giant house.

Good CEOs with a chip on their shoulder do this unintentionally, and they try to fix it by working with people like me. Bad CEOs—and other types of fear-based leaders—create deliberately unstable environments *on purpose*, then maintain them that way for their own benefit. It is a mechanism that ensures continued dominance.

Who could possibly benefit from chaos? I promise you, they do.

First, if the factions beneath them (company departments, children who will inherit the family business, etc.) are constantly warring, they can never band together to usurp the leader.

Second, when there's constant confusion, they get to be *the only source of truth in the ecosystem*. It's so confusing, and puts people so off balance, that their word essentially becomes the law of their ecosystem.

The CEOs I know who do this are also known for being deeply intense micromanagers. Projects get blocked for absolute months, because teams are not allowed to proceed even on small line items without their say-so.

This is by design. It makes them feel important. It makes them irreplaceable. And it makes the entire business totally hinge on themselves. What a way to stroke an ego!

So when you see someone generating chaos, don't mistake it for a mess. It's *calculated.* And it gives these types of leaders exactly what they need.

See it for what it is: a power play designed to exhaust you, and keep you reactive, instead of strategic. Don't fall for it. They want you confused, distracted, and defensive, because then you're easier to control.

Learn Their Buttons, Then Press the Keys: Set Strategic Traps

Sometimes, being around fear-based leaders can feel like being amongst a bunch of aliens. They seem like mysteries, because it's like the rules of physics don't apply to them.

I have often described this as throwing a ball. With most people, you throw a ball around them, and it hits the wall and bounces back. With fear-based leaders, the ball goes *through* the wall, then is eaten by a void, and you never see it again.

It's maddening. But I promise, they follow logic. So, I want to outline: What do they care about? What do they really want? What are their buttons? And what distracts them?

A basic blueprint (which does vary some from person to person) might go as follows:

They care about (on the surface):

- Money
- Power
- Fame
- Status
- Image
- Revenge
- Spite
- Dominance
- Proving people wrong
- Making people suffer, because they can
- Subjecting people to their will

What do they really want?

- To be seen and heard, and loved anyway
- For someone to genuinely care for them
- For the rest of the world to feel as dark and empty as they do inside
- For the anger and pain inside them to stop

What are their buttons?

- Insults (for all they insult others, they are *very* sensitive)

- Implications of weakness or inferiority
- Insubordination
- People not being "impressed" enough by them
- Autonomous behavior
- Critical thinking
- Laughter
- Joy
- People having different goals or values than they do
- People not taking their advice
- People not asking for their advice
- People not appropriately kowtowing, or putting them on a pedestal
- People not sucking up enough to them

What distracts them?

- Asking them about themselves
- Praising them
- Mentioning their nemeses, or people they consider incompetent or "beta"
- Making them look good to the people above them
- Pulling in favors for them
- Nodding and smiling attentively (if female) or fist-bumping (if a bro)
- Asking to see pictures of their newest shiny thing (yacht, girlfriend, etc.)
- Finding a common enemy

If you *know what they want, and know how to distract and trigger them, you can play them with masterstrokes they will never see coming.* Distractions aren't just a relief—they are leverage points. Every time you engage their ego or feed their insecurity, you divert their attention from policing or punishing you.

Give them things they care about to win favor. Suggest that nemeses are attacking things that set off their buttons. When initiatives you care about are brought up, hijack the conversation with distractions to pivot attention away from you. And so on.

What else am I missing, that you would add to this list?

Key Takeaways and Reflection Questions

Takeaways

1. Fear-based leaders trade in information. Do not share even benign things with them.
2. Being underestimated can be an asset.
3. Fear-based leaders are easily baited and distracted.
4. Fear-based leaders need consistent and constant validation.
5. Availability is leverage. Do not be constantly available.
6. Fear-based leaders think in black-and-white ways. Embrace the gray.
7. Fear-based leaders feed on attention, and intentionally destroy things to see people react strongly. Do not give them attention,

and do not react when they press your buttons.
8. Fear-based leaders believe that people are possessions, and that ownership is for a lifetime. When you try to escape their orbit, be careful, or kiss the ring on the way out.
9. If you're seeing red, do some jumping jacks, and hold something cold on your face.
10. Fear-based leaders don't negotiate fairly—so you need to level up to take them on. Expect bad-faith tactics.
11. Know what fear-based leaders are capable of giving, and you won't be disappointed.
12. Believe people's actions, not their words. When people show you who they are, believe them.
13. When you're being gaslit or brainwashed, let the fear-based leader know you're not falling for it.
14. Bend, don't snap. You are worth 100 times your fear-based leader; do not let them diminish your value.
15. Pick a few precious things wisely to prioritize.
16. Do not let yourself get too used to fear-based behavior.
17. See the space between the slats. No one can contain you without your consent.
18. You are allowed to move. Do not be afraid of getting unstuck.

19. Fear-based leaders are falsely generous. Do not believe them.
20. Diligence is critical in fear-based organizations.
21. Remembering your human imperfection is key to not letting power corrupt you.
22. Perception is a double-edged sword; see through the halos.
23. Don't allow others to tell you what you want. Marketing can be misleading.
24. If you start giving things to a fear-based leader, they will only want more.
25. Chaos is a deliberate strategy. Don't get sucked into the vortex.
26. If you know the buttons, you can press the keys. Set strategic traps for predictable fear-based leaders.

Reflection Questions

1. What information have you seen used against you?
2. How available are you to the fear-based leader in your life?
3. What calms you down the most when you're extra stressed?
4. What are the fear-based leaders around you capable of giving? What isn't in their store?

5. When is a recent time someone's actions didn't match their words? What does that say about them?
6. How many things are you trying to keep as priorities right now? Is it too many to do them all well?
7. Are you stuck? How can you get unstuck?
8. Is the generosity you see from the fear-based leader real, or false? Why or why not?
9. Whose halos are the strongest around you?
10. When have you seen intentional chaos?

Part Three

Navigating Systems and Safety

Recognizing Stalking, Safety Risks, and Control Tactics

The main part of this book has taught you how to recognize and understand fear-based leaders, and how to navigate day-to-day life with them. However, the longer you are around people like this, the more you are going to end up in *edge case scenarios*. And in those types of unexpected circumstances, it is critical that you know how to protect yourself. So, the next sections are going to be about navigating relationships with fear-based leaders out in the real world—where often, both legal and safety needs come into play.

I never expected to become an expert in this—but due to a range of surprising circumstances I have encountered around powerful, unethical people, I have had to deal with lawsuits, surveillance, law enforcement, media, journalists, and more.

Many fear-based leaders have a low distress tolerance. They are brittle and inflexible, and when things take them by surprise, they often fly into rages. For some of them, that comes with risks to your physical safety—they may just scream at and deride their team, but others are prone to physically throwing things, grabbing or assaulting others, or intimidation tactics. Others prefer more subtle forms of abuse—mind games, intimidation, or fear tactics. But that's what this is—abuse can happen in public or professional spaces just as much as it can happen in a home.

Most people assume that if they follow the rules, they'll be safe. That if they're good, honest, and diligent, they'll be spared harm. But predators don't target rule breakers—they target rule followers, especially the ones who can't imagine bending the rules themselves, and therefore can't imagine that others might do so with impunity. Those people are easy to disarm. Easy to trap. Easy to shame into silence. If you're wondering whether this applies to you—whether the unease you've been feeling is something more—this piece is for you, and here I will be your guide.

In every single important relationship and job I have ever had—with the exception of the companies I started myself—I have seen illegal behavior affect me or someone I know. And I know better than anyone, as someone who has been in multiple relationships involving domestic violence, that it's the people who are close to you that are dangerous—not so often a stranger in a dark alley. People like this will tell you how safe you are, how lucky you are to be with them, then slap you, just to keep you disoriented and controllable.

As the child of abjectly cruel, controlling people, who does advocacy work outside of my day job, I have personally been stalked, blackmailed, kidnapped, physically and sexually assaulted, financially controlled, brainwashed, reputationally smeared, isolated, ostracized, groomed, and more. Family members, friends, and professional contacts of mine have been murdered, hacked, followed, harassed, molested, drugged, raped, sued, and blackballed.

But, I have survived—in fact, I'm happy, loving, gentle, and caring as well as strong, assertive, and confident. So I'm going to teach you so that you can be vigilant, aware, and prepared, but not live life in fear.

First, you need to learn to recognize when you're at risk. Here are some common situations to watch for:

1. **The persona non grata (i.e., the professional fade and push out):** When companies or organizations don't like an employee, they have a few options—a) fire the person, which opens the door for wrongful termination claims, b) drum up reasons to put the person on a performance improvement plan (PIP) that creates some legal cover of poor performance, or c) go for a classic fade. The first two

are pretty straightforward, but the third does not get enough coverage.

In a fade and push out, a company starts to slowly isolate and ostracize an employee. They give them a little bit less work every week, cut them out of one more meeting per month, whisper in the background to other employees that they're political kryptonite, and start taking away things like one-on-ones, feedback, and stakeholder relationships, to slowly frustrate the person until the person voluntarily decides to leave. This creates the largest amount of legal coverage, and often leaves people more willing to sign mutual separation clauses that include nondisparagement agreements (which in most cases are not actually legally enforceable in the US). It's a little bit like gaslighting—the person feels vaguely less and less included, until they believe they're no longer a fit for the organization.

Don't fall for this. This set of tactics works best on people who are afraid of authority, strongly respect hierarchy, and derive most of their purpose/meaning from one organization. If you're not afraid of them, and don't mind having more time to yourself, you can wait them out and then leave on your terms.

2. **Speaking truth to power:** This is not an intimidation tactic—it's a trigger for them. Anytime that you speak truth to a powerful figure—most especially in a public forum—it turns you into a major target. So if you're going to do this, batten down your security hatches first, and only use your real name if you have to.
3. **Physical safety risks:** If you see someone break items, it's not a stretch for them to break people. The people who smash phones, break a tennis racket, or throw a golf club will often smash your face if you're sitting close enough during a rage. *Avoid being in private spaces with people like this.*
4. **Stalking:** This one deserves a bit of a deep dive, because someone following you is only about 10% of what stalking means. SPARC, a stalking awareness organization, defines stalking behaviors as falling into the following categories:
    a. **Surveillance**—this can be in person or digital, and involves watching and gathering information about someone. It can include seeking information about you from friends or family, accessing your online accounts, putting a GPS tracker on you, using

tracking software on your phone, or monitoring online activity.
b. **Life invasion**—this means showing up in someone's life without their consent. It can include unwanted calls, texts, messages, sending unwanted gifts or objects, spreading rumors, impersonating you online, deliberately humiliating you in public, or showing up at places you go.
c. **Intimidation**—this can include threats to you or those you care about, blackmail, threatening to post photos of you, engaging in symbolic violence, threatening to harm themself, or deliberately frightening you.
d. **Interference**—disrupting the victim's life by impacting their reputation, employment, or safety. This can include stealing property, disrupting your work or social life, keeping you from leaving places, assaulting you, or sharing private information or photos of/about you with others.

For stalking, there are legal recourses. I have had to apply for a protective order before, and it isn't fun—but it can guarantee police response time in just a few minutes, and it is *always* better to be safe than sorry.

5. **Coercive control:** This is a type of pattern of controlling behaviors that make people feel forced to do what the abuser wants. Here are some of the signs of it (by J. Hill):
    a. Isolating you from your support system.
    b. Monitoring your activity throughout the day.
    c. Denying you freedom and autonomy ("No, you can't go to your kid's play"; "No, you can't go out to grab lunch").
    d. Gaslighting.
    e. Name-calling and severe criticism.
    f. Limiting access to money and controlling finances (this does not get talked about in work relationships enough—it can be just as abusive for a manager to cut off resources or hold them as a carrot/stick at work as it can be for an abusive spouse to do it at home).
    g. Forcing you to take care of all of a role's duties.
    h. Turning others, especially dependents like minors or direct reports, against you.
    i. Controlling aspects of your health or body ("No, you can't go to the doctor today"; "I want all my female

employees to have long hair and wear dresses").

j. Making jealous accusations about the time you spend with others ("I know you'd rather be working on this project with Marco, but I guess you're stuck with me").

k. Threatening those you care about (kids, pets, etc.—e.g., "If you don't get this report done, you can kiss that trip to your son's graduation goodbye").

6. **Intimidation:** Covered partially above, this is doing anything that makes you feel afraid in order to make you alter your behavior.

7. **Harassment:** Intentionally causing distress through repeated antagonistic behaviors.

Study this list well. It could end up saving you, or someone else, a lot of suffering.

Whatever you do, do not bury your head in the sand. Too many people live in a world of wishful thinking. If you see warning signs of the behaviors above, *wake up*. If you see these things happening to the people around you, do not think it could never happen to you. *Always have an exit plan of where you would go, or what you would do, if things go south.*

Archetypes of Half-Safe Controllers

In addition to spotting behaviors, I am also going to teach you how to spot some of the common types of controlling people.

If someone asked you who is the most dangerous of safe, half-safe, or unsafe people, you'd probably guess unsafe, right?

This is actually incorrect. Unsafe people are an easy choice—if you see that they're always likely to harm you, then you don't spend time around them. It's the *half-safe people*—the ones who are sometimes dangerous, sometimes safe—who end up causing the most damage. Because your brain *wants* to think the best of someone, to see their good side, and believe they're better than they are, which lulls people into staying longer than is healthy—and because you never know if you're going to get a metaphorical hug, or be punched, so you have to walk on eggshells. That type of constant tenterhooks does major damage to your stress hormones, and immune system.

You might think, "I would never fall for that. I have zero tolerance for bad behavior." And that might be true. But I know a lot of smart people who have fallen for this type of bad-boy leader. Here are some common ones to watch for:

The Saint
(Covert Abuser with a Public Halo)

Traits: This person appears generous, even progressive, to the outside world, but behind closed doors, uses shame, guilt, or confusion as control tactics. They confuse their targets because everyone else who knows them in a public capacity raves about how they're an angel on earth.

Impact: Their public image can be weaponized to protect them, and to make potential discontented employees gaslight themselves. They are most likely to abuse people they have direct power over (e.g., employees, children).

Where you'll find them: Disaster relief nonprofit CEO, war zone doctor, handsome CEO.

The Martyr
(Control Through Guilt)

Traits: Positions themself as self-sacrificing, and controls others by saying things like, "After everything I've done for you, and you can't even . . ."

Impact: Uses shame, obligation, and "you owe me" dynamics to enforce compliance.

Where you'll find them: Family businesses, cofounder relationships, manager-employee relationships.

The Proxy Punisher
(Control Through Delegation)

Traits: Enlists others to harm you, rather than doing it themselves, then, hides behind deniability (e.g., "I didn't tell them to hurt you, I just made it clear that I was disappointed. It's not my fault they took it too far").

Impact: Creates a chilling environment with no blood on their hands.

Where you'll find them: Billionaire power games, the financial sector, politics, and senior leadership.

The Golden Ball and Chain
(Control Through Dependency)

Traits: Provides initially generous support, opportunity, or access—in exchange for your feudal pledge.
Impact: Makes targets feel like they can't leave, because it's shameful, or they'd be worse off because of it (and they feel like they "owe" the leader).
Where it shows up: Mentor-protégé relationships.

The Benevolent Mentor

Traits: Seems like a wise, altruistic leader, until your growth threatens them or they move to extract value from you.
Impact: Leaves targets feeling abandoned, confused, and lacking agency.
Where it shows up: Most common between opposite-gendered leaders and their reports.

Can you see why these may create mixed feelings? Take some time, and think about it. And if you take away anything, let it be that control can wear many masks. Some tactics are obvious, but many are dressed as generosity, opportunity, or guilt.

Guide to Physical Safety

I have been trained in physical safety by people who are ex–intelligence services. Not everyone can afford that—and so I am going to outline a few strategies that could work for almost anyone here.

All of this is common sense—and also, part of being aware. You don't have to be paranoid—you need to be mindful.

1. **Do not give away personal information easily:** The easiest ways to exploit you happen because you have given away information to someone you should not. And too often, it's because of new people who show up in your life that just seem "too friendly" or "too interested." To help with this:

a. Use a virtual mailbox on all documentation related to the fear-based leader, instead of your home address. If they're your employer, they don't need to know where you live.
b. Use a service like Google Voice for a second phone number that is not your real number, for all vendors like DoorDash, grocery delivery, etc.
c. Use a throwaway email for all stores/accounts.
d. Do not use your real birthday in sign-ups.
e. Do not geotag your social media posts. If you must post photos of a vacation, *do it after you're home again, not while you're there.*
f. Create a "Starbucks name" (not your real name)—make this your name for all delivery apps, restaurant reservations, Yelp reviews, etc.
g. Set all social media and email accounts to max privacy. Be sure to test what the accounts look like when not logged in to see what's still showing. Do not use your full name on social media—use a middle name instead of a last name, or a nickname, and remember that all photos of you can be scraped and searched to turn up related accounts.

2. **Install indoor and outdoor security cameras:** Make sure that they are not accessible by the leader—for example, if they have friends in law enforcement, do not use cloud-based solutions that are subject to warrantless surveillance access. You may also need to take plates off your car, because in many jurisdictions cars are geotagged as they pass scanners. Put a "dog bell" on your entry and exit doors so that there is always noise when people enter or exit.
3. **Be street smart:** Do not go dark places, where there are no security cameras, alone at night. If you can afford it, adopt a dog.
4. **Make backups:** Always have printed copies of your IDs, birth certificate, and critical prescriptions at home and ready to go if needed. Back up critical data, photographs, or recordings in multiple places (both physical hard drives and cloud).
5. **Always have an exit plan:** If you suddenly can't go home, or to the office, always know where you would go. If you think you're going to be in a meeting where you may be unsafe, always have an excuse ready to leave. *Do not get into the car with fear-based leaders.* They love having captive audiences, and they love seeing people's reactions when they take you to places you didn't want to go. Drive yourself

instead, or take public transit. Tell people you're getting in steps, or whatever you need to.

6. **Always identify exits:** When you visit a new space—a restaurant, concert, etc.—always scan entrances, exits, and crowd behavior. When you travel, be aware of publicly accessible secure spaces (hotels, police stations, hospitals, embassies) near you.
7. **Do not drink heavily or do drugs:** It's much more easy to harm you if you're in a vulnerable state.
8. **Vary your routines:** Switch up your commute route, departure and arrival times, and routines each week.
9. **Keep emergency supplies:** Always make sure you have a flashlight near where you sleep. Keep significant cash on hand. Have a hard copy of emergency contact information near you.

Guide to Cyber Security

1. **Prevent ratting:** "Remote access technology" allows your camera or microphone to be hacked and turned on at will, with no notification. Put sliding covers over your cameras on your phone and computer, and buy mic locks (plugs that block your phone and computer's headphone ports so they cannot be activated). When you travel, use Faraday bags (which enclose devices to block hacking/duplication).
2. **Use safe providers:** It matters where your tech is located. Many fear-based leaders have friends in law enforcement, which in many countries have warrantless surveillance powers (even Google, Apple, and Meta must give back-end access to government requests). So choose providers like Proton and Tuta, which

are based in jurisdictions like Switzerland, or messaging apps like Signal (which has special encryption) to host sensitive communications, financial data, or legal information. Never link a backup to your real identity (e.g., don't have your real Gmail recovery link to a Proton alias).

3. **Turn off location services:** Go into your phone settings and make sure that every application is set to "do not track" when it comes to your location.
4. **Turn on two-factor authentication:** The best way to do this is to use physical security keys, like YubiKeys.
5. **Always use a VPN and a secure DNS:** Your metadata, OS, IP, and logins leave fingerprints. Use a strong VPN, DNS, and EDR, and for sensitive data transfers, use browsers like Brave with Tor enabled. Do not let your passwords be saved in browser key chains.
6. **Be aware of metadata:** Strip metadata (author names, location data) from PDFs, Word docs, and photos before sending or posting. If you have Lockdown Mode enabled on your phone, it will stop logging the location of photographs.
7. **Set up contingency plans:** If you have sensitive data, legal action, or insider knowledge, set up what's called a "deadman's switch."

It's essentially technology in which if you do not reply in a certain interval (e.g., a week), it assumes that something has happened to you, and it sends whatever you have instructed it to to specified recipients (journalists, lawyers, etc.).

Remember that it's often safer to blend in, than to disappear. It's less suspicious to have your phone and computer data patterns be very boring, than to have all activity die.

If You're Asked to Do Something Illegal . . .

Play dumb. "You don't mean that I should give Johnie advance notice of the merger, right? Because I know you'd never suggest something illegal, and that's insider trading."

"Oh, you meant for me to tell Tim that he had to drop the lawsuit or we'd tank his startup IPO? I thought you just meant I should ask him."

The fear-based leader already thinks they're the only competent one in the room. *Play into that.* They will assume that you're just being a fool because that's what you were to start with. They understand weaponized incompetence very well—but they're so arrogant that they would never think of someone trying that on them.

The most classic societal example of this is when a wife asks her husband to load the dishwasher, but he does such a bad job, making a huge mess, that she gives up on having him do it again, and does it herself. *That's what you want the leader to do—give up and do it themself.* Be their fool, not their goon.

You can also report to government agencies or authorities—but keep in mind that becoming a CI or witness carries risks, and that fear-based leaders often have connections in high places (as any leader does). If at any point knowledge of what the leader is doing, or not standing up to them, could be deemed complicit behavior to a crime, leave the organization immediately. Tell the world you need to go care for a sick relative, or that your marriage is going through a rough patch and you need to work less—whatever you need to say to get out. True lackeys would go to jail to protect the leader—but that's not you.

How to Find, Select, Pitch, and Retain Lawyers

People who work for, or spend time around, fear-based leaders are often surprised to find themselves interacting with the legal system. But, the longer you're in contact with this kind of person, the higher the likelihood you will end up there.

Why? Because they frequently either do illegal things *to* you, or ask you to do illegal things *for* them. They don't see themselves as criminals, just as wealthy people don't see themselves as unethical for using tax havens. Instead, they simply think that they are above the rules.

I am not normally self-indulgent in my writing, and I wrote this book as fast as I could, because the world's need for the information pressed urgency upon me. But this chapter was the one that I put off writing until the very end.

Why? Because *I do not like having to think about all of my experiences with lawyers.*

That should tell you something about what it is to interact with those in the legal profession. As someone related to multiple lawyers, I know that many lawyers are good people. And yet, I want you to understand from the very beginning that anything to do with the legal system is going to feel *like running uphill with weights on your back in a storm.*

I have worked with lawyers extensively for decades. I have had to retain lawyers or navigate the court system on double-digit separate matters related to my advocacy work, life, and health, and in many, many work engagements related to M&A or regulatory affairs. In the past year alone, I pitched over ninety law firms to find the best counsels for important cases (which is about the same amount of effort it takes to pitch and close a startup venture round).

Just like with fear-based leaders, I need you to understand the *mind and incentives* of a lawyer, so that you understand how you will be pushed or persuaded by potential counsels.

Some of this may sound harsh—but I promise you, it is based on my experiences with hundreds of lawyers in multiple countries, across many different types of law.

1. **Lawyers are risk-averse creatures.** Lawyers are trained to spot liability and risk. This means that they see danger at every single

turn—and they do not like betting on uncertain outcomes. This means that they frequently decline good cases just because they see small margins of failure. If it's not 90% certain, to them it's a loss. This is the opposite of how venture capital and startups work, so it is especially hard for tech leaders to understand.

2. **They are trained to see clients as irritating, emotional sheep.** Despite the fact that you are the one paying them, and you have the power to fire them, most lawyers do not respect, like, or appreciate their clients. They see the clients as annoying, variable, illogical necessities to handhold, browbeat, and manipulate into what they want.

3. **Their incentives are rarely aligned with yours.** Lawyers care about a few things—fame, money, time, and promotion. If *you* want to settle a case quietly, but *they* think a public trial could make their career, then they may sabotage negotiations without telling you. If *they* signed up for too many simultaneous cases and need more time back, they might tell you that your odds of receiving a better settlement are low—when in reality, that's subjective. This is why it's *critical to write an interview guide for every intake call*

in which you grill each potential counsel on their specialties, context, and priorities.

4. **They have massive egos.** For one case this past year, I pitched sixty-five firms. Out of all of those firms, all in the plaintiff-side space that I needed, *only three read the law and facts correctly.* This is despite me sending them full outlines of the facts, all of the relevant case law, and sitting in approximately six hours of interviews with each firm I spoke with. Despite almost all of them being objectively wrong, *every single one was confident that they were right.* And yet, I had them tell me that my case was worth everywhere from $0 to $50,000,000, with every possible quote in between.

5. **Most use case molds, rather than doing original thinking.** It might be confusing to try to understand why a third of counsels told me my case was worth nothing, a third told me it was worth $2M, and the rest were all over the map. But I know why this is true—and that is because the firms use *case molds*. Lawyers develop heuristics over time, like "all toxic tort cases are worth $500K" or "all severance disputes are worth $2M" or "all cases in which an employee has not been fired cannot be settled for meaningful dollar value." Evaluating based on real facts takes

time, and energy, *so they don't*. Instead, they skim relevant information, then apply a *case mold* that spits out the value—*even if they're extremely wrong*.

6. **Solo shops ≠ big firms.** This is where deciding between solo shops and big firms comes into play. Big firms are scarier, mightier against an opponent. They have major resources in case they get data dumped with hundreds of thousands of files. But, they are extremely rigid—in the types of cases they accept, and in their enforcement of case molds. To get around this, you can use a solo shop attorney—an attorney who runs their own firm—but you need to understand the trade-offs. Solo shop attorneys are often people who are extremely smart, but who did not like the rigidity of large firm life. They are often more custom, creative thinkers, who can work with you in a more humanistic, customer-centric way. However, many of them left big law and went out on their own because they *don't play nice with others*. This can mean they are more prickly, or more defensive, than big firm lawyers who are being held accountable for their behavior by their partnerships. *If something goes wrong with a solo shop attorney, you cannot call their boss. You have to find new counsel.* But, I would

argue that things are *more likely* to go wrong with a big firm in the first place—because they see you as a dollar sign, not a person.

7. **Litigators ≠ pre-litigation specialists.** In general, when you bring a claim, you have to decide whether you want to *settle* or whether you want to *go to trial*. In a settlement, you might directly negotiate with the defendant, or do a one- or two-day mediation to reach an agreement. The whole thing often stays confidential, and matters resolve typically within one year depending on mediator schedules. In a trial, the resolution can take multiple years, and it's public, splashy, messy, and time consuming for all parties—and a judge or jury decides the outcome, not you and the defendant. Attorneys specialize typically in either one or the other. *You need to decide early which you want to go with—do you want the quiet ease of a settlement? Or do you want the empowerment and challenge of a public meat grinder of a trial?* This is important to know early, because *pre-litigation attorneys are supposed to be nimble, subtle, strategic, and a light touch.* Litigators are *burn-down-the-house hammers who oversimplify legal arguments so that they make sense to a jury of laypeople. You do not want a litigator for pre-litigation—they could jeopardize the whole*

negotiation by being an unmitigated asshole. And you do not want a pre-litigation specialist for the drama of court. In general, the pre-litigation attorney's fee is between 20 and 40%. A litigator's fee is typically more around 40%.

8. **Class lawyers ≠ individual lawyers.** The next thing you need to understand is class versus individual. If you are in a large group of people who have been harmed—like if half your colleagues have been discriminated against—you have a choice. You can file a claim as an individual, or as a class. If you file as an individual, you often get more money, and your case settles years faster. If you file as a class, you get less money, and it takes longer, but it can garner more press, or push for more systemic change. *Attorneys will often try to push you into leading a class, because they make a ton more money in class suits than individual suits.* To get around this, either choose firms that do not do class work, or state unequivocally in intake if you do not want to form a class. Be firm.

9. **They will pressure test you.** Attorneys want to know if you're strong enough for a legal fight—so they will often deliberately abuse you in order to see how you take it. In my calls with lawyers, I have been told that I'm weak, that I'm not strong enough for trial, that

I don't know what I'm talking about, that I'm wrong, that the defendant is right, that I have no business being in the suit to begin with, that my demands are a lot of work so I should give up, and on five separate occasions, that I am just like the lawyer's teenage/college-age daughters.

10. **They will try to squash you to make you easier to control.** If they sense that you are tough like me—in that I am direct, firm, and know what I want—they will often try to beat you down, in order to get you to acquiesce to their strategy. Do not let them do this.

11. **If you don't fit into a box, you threaten them.** Attorneys have massive egos—and they are universally terrified of clients who are smarter than they are. I have had people ghost me, yell at me, write me multipage emails trying to put me in my place, and try to repeatedly box me out of my own cases. Be patient. Soothe their bruised egos. Tell them how important they are. But stand up for your needs. Be consistent, insistent, warm, and polite. Be the role model of how they should be behaving.

12. **Most lawyers are analysts, not strategists.** Lawyers think small. They are all about brittle logic, tiny rules and laws, and often totally miss the big picture. In my experience, only

5% of lawyers have any sense of business strategy. This means that you need to set your own strategy, and be clear with them about what you want.

13. **They won't tell you about taxes.** Attorneys suck at numbers. They suck at finance in general. So don't expect them to pay attention to your financial needs. This means that if you're in a high-dollar-value case, *it is your responsibility to find a tax counsel early.* They need to be involved in reviewing demand letter drafts or settlement terms, because they can save you literally millions of dollars in taxes, based on whether the defendant pays your legal fees to your lawyer, or to you, and on demand category allocation.

Pick counsel selection criteria before you start outreach. I always seek someone who treats me with mutual respect, genuinely believes me, and sees me as a strategic thought partner. Maybe you want a bulldog or someone who settles quickly. It's up to you—but beware of the trade-offs—bulldogs don't always know how to turn it off with their clients, and may bite you as much as the opposition. Quick settlers may leave money on the table. And so on.

Once you have decided what type of lawyer you need (plaintiff/defense, big firm/solo, individual/class, and specialty), you will need to pitch them.

Almost every lawyer does what's called an intake, in which they ask you the facts, and try to decide whether you'll be a good client. Half of the firms use useless specialists on the phone who know nothing about the law—and those specialists make mistakes.

Instead, email or LinkedIn message the name partners of the firm directly in an email explaining the merits of your case, the expected dollar value, and a request to meet with them. Attach:

- A case summary of facts, timeline, and relevant law (use an LLM to research this)
- The questions you have for them as your potential counsel
- The timeline in which you'd like the case resolved

Then, use every single intake to grill each firm on the same set of questions. (What is their focus? What would their strategy be? How many cases like this do they do a year? Which lawyer would be assigned to you? What is their contingency fee or retainer rate? etc.)

Take notes on each call with each counsel (if possible, use a virtual meeting or phone recorder if you are in a single-party consent state). Write down how they make you feel, how seriously they took you, what unique perspectives they offered.

With every single call, adjust your pitch based on their reactions so that it starts to more and more anticipate the questions that you will be asked in advance (if it's being bucketed too small, right size it; if they're dumping you into a bias box—e.g., all plaintiffs say their industry is reputation sensitive—*lean against it hard* in every single conversation). *Show them you're prepared. Show them you're serious.*

Expect that there will be a funnel at play here. You may need to pitch ten firms, of which three will be interested in deeper intake, and then you may have two to choose from.

Sometimes, you end up having to take a patronizing, diminutive lawyer, because they are the only ones available, like in one of my cases—but I let him see me as a malleable victim, because it worked to my advantage for him to see me as a poor little girl who was wronged by a mean, bad doctor, and that narrative can be compelling for a settlement. If your lawyer sees you as a malleable victim, and that makes them fight harder in a way that maximizes your win, then fine—let them play their little hero fantasy. But that should not have to be the answer for most people.

After you choose who you want, you'll have to "redline" or edit your fee agreement. This is when you can negotiate on price. If your case is simple or you've done a lot of research or evidence collection already, push for a 5 to 10 percent reduction in fees. Make sure you get in writing that you'll be consulted on all settlement offers and involved in strategy throughout, and that you will have redline rights on all major documents. Insist on regular updates (one to two times a month at least), and on monthly ledgers being sent with case costs, to keep them mindful of how much they're spending on your account.

After that, it's up to you—but remember that if your lawyer isn't serving you, you have the right to find alternate counsel at any time.

When Part of Your Tool Kit Gets Taken Away

Fear-based leaders often punish through *austerity*.

They are far more likely to *take things away*—make deadlines too tight, make resources too thin—than they are to be too generous. This is why Mark Zuckerberg created a "year of efficiency" in 2023, firing tons of people just to hire them back again. You will often hear terms tossed around like "lean teams" or "doing more with less."

And so, I want to talk to you about how to cope with losing things that you consider completely crucial to your success.

I am really familiar with this, because as a consultant I ran procurement negotiations, M&A cuts, and private equity diligences, and in VC and startups I have run many exercises to extend runway during times in which fundraising is more difficult.

But by far, the harshest lessons I have ever been subject to regarding the loss of a tool kit have been with my health. For many years, I lost access to many parts of myself and my abilities, never knowing whether I would see them ever again.

I have had seven traumatic brain injuries, in addition to a genetic condition that caused severe brain atrophy.

In the months after acute concussions, I lost access to my depth perception and peripheral vision. I would fall off curbs, and I constantly walked into doorframes. I was not allowed to drive for months. I could not do abstract conceptual problem solving, or picture the things I read in books anymore. At one point, my IQ was down by 40 percent, and there were months where I could only handle an hour a day on screens.

But what's really interesting is *how I chose to cope*. You might think it would be hard to get through life in those states (and it was brutal to suddenly have limits I'd never experienced before)—but not only did I get through it, I worked high-powered jobs, made new friends, moved, completed medical treatments, and still kept living. My rule of thumb has always been that as long as I can be outside and feel the sun on my face, life is worth living.

So how did I do it? I used creative problem solving, and applied the theory of spoons.

In chronic illness circles, the theory of spoons goes that the average person might have forty spoons to spend on their daily activities. It takes a spoon to get ready in the morning, three spoons to make breakfast, and a spoon to go to work.

Someone with difficult health conditions might only get five spoons, because they have fatigue, pain, or other limitations that severely limit their ability to perform tasks.

I spent a lot of time in a five-spoons situation. So I worked creatively to offload every single task that I could to technology, rigging elaborate systems of Alexa and Siri reminders, and learned to ruthlessly prioritize how to spend spoons. What other people might call *myopic*, I think of as *relentless focus*.

I became very, very efficient—and also extremely good at classifying tasks as critical, nice to have, and someday. This is how I was able to write this book in eight weeks while working full time, moving, training a service dog, and completing medical treatments.

And I know that if and when fear-based leaders cut your budget, take away your PTO, or otherwise take away things that you have always felt were critical—you are going to be capable of adapting, too.

Start by figuring out what was taken, and what the function of that line item was. Then, start outlining the consequences of not having it. Can anything substitute? Can you borrow something from another team? Can you take on outside funding or sponsors? Can your community work together to form a net to cover the hole that was created? Can you do a hackathon to make an internal version of what the vendor provided? Can you get interns to do it? Can you funnel resources from somewhere else without people noticing?

Then think about what is truly the most critical and important. What are you going to protect at all costs? What can your initiative not live without?

Any person who has a family and has lived paycheck to paycheck is going to be familiar with this dance. You can deal without food, but not without heat. It will also be familiar to anyone who has worked in a field medical setting in war zones or refugee camps. Can a pen be a tracheal tube? And so on.

It's not fun. It really sucks. Not being able to be myself for years is not something I would wish on anyone. But it was *survivable*—and sometimes, survive is what you most need to do in environments like this—help get the team through tornado season with as few casualties as possible, and then work together to rebuild another day.

When You Lose It All and Have to Start Over

Sometimes, you are able to protect what matters most to you in systems led by leaders like this—but that can come at a very high cost. And sometimes, you have to call it quits, and start over again, leaving with just the most important things: your life, your loved ones, and your values.

I know this much better than most people. In my life, due to random acts of God, I have had to lose my home and almost all my possessions four times. I also had to leave 90 percent of my family behind when I came out, and then had to leave my city behind when I became unsafe there.

The first three times I lost my home, it felt like my world was ending. It was gut-wrenching, miserable, and I was deeply, deeply upset.

But guess what? By the fourth time, I wasn't happy

about it—but I had practice. I knew in my bones that I knew how to start over. I knew that I would create home wherever I went—because I build community, and create comfort wherever I am. I knew that my possessions, while lovely, were less important than my life, than my wellbeing, than being able to be myself fully, and live my values.

And, I had also learned that things that initially seem bad are not always what they appear.

I grew up in a horrible environment, and I've worked at many challenging places—but because of that, I knew how to write this book.

I have intense health conditions—but because I do, I have the knowledge and empathy to design clinical trials for them, mentor startups in that space, and create advocacy, lobbying, and awareness initiatives that are going to help millions more people get correctly diagnosed.

I didn't want to leave my last home at all; I was planning on building a house nearby and raising children there. But, when all of a sudden I had to move cities, it gave me a sudden chance to redo my finances, my tech, my friendships, my home, my neighborhood, and my area, while launching a career more focused on what I love.

How many times in your life do you get a slate wiped clean like that? A chance to rebuild purely from a place of intention? *I'm so lucky that I had to leave my home. I'm so lucky that I have genetic illnesses. I'm so lucky that I know how to start over whenever I need to.*

Just like me, you are creative, resourceful, and whole.[1]

---

1. Tenet of Co-Active Coaching.

Sometimes things in your life that seem bad on the surface are redirections towards a higher purpose. And sometimes, they just super suck. But often, when things really suck, your capacity expands, you learn to triage, and what's really important becomes even more clear. If this happens to you, please remember:

1. Adaptability is your friend. Prioritize ruthlessly, and focus on the top three things that matter to you.
2. Lean on your relationships. It takes a village not just to raise a child, but to be a human.
3. Ask for help. When in doubt, make a list of what you need. Then, make a list of who might be able to provide that type of support/service/item.
4. Figure out what opportunities exist in having the slate wiped clean, and what new paths might unfold in front of you.
5. Even as the places and faces around you change, home is where you and the people you love are.

Deciding Who to Trust

Not everyone thinks the way you do. Given the same situation, people might choose to respond in ten-plus different ways. This is due to a couple of things: different pattern recognition/reactiveness based on life experiences, and different core values.

In a business, core values help people decide what to do when leaders aren't present. If a company always puts customers first, then someone would choose to resolve a customer complaint before an employee dispute. If someone values being fast, over being fair, customer service agents may try to be responsive, rather than just. And so on.

People are a little bit different. We all have core values (I shared some of mine at the beginning of this book). But rather than allowing employees to make different choices based on core values like a company does, each person's core values help them determine how to act in situations they have not encountered before. You may never have had your suitcase stolen at the airport before—but if your top value is respect, you likely won't yell at the airline about it. If on the other hand your top value is fighting for what you deserve—well, it's likely to be a different story.

I bring this up because it is relevant to who you decide to trust while working or existing in the realm of a fear-based leader. You should assume that 80 percent of people will not have the same core values that you do. When values diverge, sharing things that make you vulnerable, or open you up to risk becomes dangerous.

For example, I have had to whistleblow about how corporations were impacting the public in dangerous ways on three separate occasions, each time putting myself at risk. *However,* I learned very quickly that 90 percent of people I interacted with about these issues *did not care about public harms,* and in fact desired to *harm me for bringing these issues to light.*

So how do you know if someone shares your values?

I recommend breadcrumbing.

Breadcrumbing means tossing out benign test facts, in order to gauge a response.

> **Here's an example:** I had a medical provider's office in which I kept noticing dangerous prescriber errors, and that one of the doctors was constantly hitting on the female patients. Rather than immediately report the errors, I "test lobbed" light

feedback instead, to see how they would respond (in this case, reporting billing errors and asking for assistance).

In response, the team was defensive, angry, and a doctor called me and yelled at me for twenty minutes about how difficult and unreasonable I was for reporting the billing errors.

Verdict: This environment was *not safe for me to report further more serious errors.*

In social situations with colleagues, friends, or family, *do not assume they share your values. Breadcrumb instead.*

You could say something like, "How are you feeling about Steve's M&A plan?" If they say they're skeptical, then you go ahead and share your doubts. If they tell you Steve's plan is the only path forward—well, probably not the right venue for your worries.

Or, you might say to a relative, "Does anything seem different about Jeannie to you lately?" to see if they're open to discussing your concern about a struggling relative. If they defensively say, "No, she's doing great, why do you ask?" Then you could pivot to something innocuous, like, "She looks great; did she change her hair or get her teeth whitened?" If they say, "Yes, I'm so worried about her," then you could go ahead and share that you're worried she might be depressed.

It's tempting to think that just because you spend a lot

of time around your coworkers or family that they share your values. But, for many people, that's not the case—in fear-based ecosystems, people might share your concerns or vulnerabilities to blackmail you, gaslight you, trade as gossip for favors from others, and more. It never, ever hurts to test the waters first—so dip your toes in slowly, and keep an eye out for sharks.

When Relationships Don't Fit Right Anymore

Fear-based leaders can cause rapid change—rapid, self-serving change that does not take into account the humanity in the systems that they oversee. I used to see this all the time at in consulting, where part of my job was explaining to rash CEOs why it's often more expensive to fire, then rehire people after a merger than it is to just keep employees on the books through the merge, then train them to meet the new growth demands.

Leaders like this are prone to RIFs, hostile takeovers, arbitrary firings, incendiary lawsuits, extralegal actions, and shortsighted, inept strategies.

Being tied to someone like that—essentially, a human wrecking ball rolling around an organization—is uncomfortable. It's like a less pleasant version of my very hyper puppy trying to run into traffic, with me attached.

And something that people really do not talk about enough is that going on a journey like that—one filled with adversity—is going to change you. For some people, it makes them bitter. But for many people, it makes them grow. It clarifies what really matters to them. For the best leaders in the wings, it *sharpens* them, turning them into precision blades that are able to slice through systems to achieve their aims.

But all of this changes your lens a great deal. It may be harder for you to be patient. It may mean you need more time by yourself to process the hurt you feel at having to exist in an abrasive world. And it will absolutely change the way you see the people around you.

I can give you some examples. When I became immunocompromised, I had many friends who couldn't be bothered to stay away from me when they were sick with things like the flu. Then, as a result, I would get deathly ill, and have to go through months of expensive IV infusions to recover. Those friends couldn't care less about how it affected me, even as they saw me exhausted, ill, and struggling to recover from the intensive medical treatments. *I saw a side of them that I had never seen before—one that showed me that their convenience and comfort mattered more to them than my safety.* As a result, we are no longer close friends.

When I last visited my familial home, I was there because I was trying to help some children in my family get out of an abusive and neglectful situation by working with CPS. *I was the only one out of sixty family members who cared enough about the children to make sure they had access to food, medical care, and education.* Combined with my family's other forms of cruelty, it showed me how very different I am from them, and I started working on building my own family, instead.

You are not me, so your experiences are going to be different than mine, but know that if it suddenly feels like the people you normally spend time with are like an itchy sweater a size too small—that's normal. It's okay to want something different. It's okay to want something more. You deserve people who can bear witness to your journey, and your struggle, and see both your strength, and your potential.

Safeguarding Your Energy

You might think your most precious resource is your money, or your time, or your connections. But, all of those things require your energy in order to be valuable.

Fear-based leaders are like giant, sucking energy drains, creating a whirling vortex grabbing and consuming the energy of those around them. So, it's absolutely critical that you guard your energy fiercely, just like you would protect a child in harm's way. Without your energy, you are unable to help, unable to protect, unable to fully be.

Start this process by taking note of every interaction you have in a five-day period. After each one, write down whether you feel more energized, neutral, or drained afterwards. Then, boost the types of activities that fill you up, and cut the things that drain you. Be ruthless. You don't have to see a friend who's a downer just because of tradition—your wellbeing is *always* more important than societal expectations.

Pick four identities you want to invest in, to make sure you are shoring up aspects of yourself, in preparation for a fear-based leader to try to take away the identity you have in their sphere (e.g., being a VP or senior leader at work). Name the identity, then make a commitment to how you're going to honor it. For identities that boost you, this can mean adding time. For identities that drain you, it means setting limits. This might look like:

- I am a potter. I spend two nights a week making ceramics.
- I am a godmother. I see my godchildren twice a month for sleepovers.
- I am a dog mom. I am the best owner in the history of my dog's life.
- I am a senior leader at my job. I only work from 9 a.m. to 7 p.m. each day.

You know who the problematic entities in your life are—the ones who won't take no for an answer, make everything about themselves, or sign you up for things without asking your permission.

Practice protective phrases in the mirror every day for a week that put hard limits on their requests. Do it in a voice that's natural to you. Examples:

- I'm sorry, I'm not available to help you this weekend.

- No, I can't do that; you will need to find someone else.
- I need to get off the phone now.
- I only have ten minutes to speak with you . . . I am going to leave now.
- No, I will not be doing that.
- I'm going to have to ask you to leave now.
- I appreciate the thought, but that's not a good fit for me right now.

You only have one you. Always put your oxygen mask on first. You come before your kids, your spouse, your pets. If you pour out your cup for them and leave nothing for yourself to drink, you will die of thirst and then you can never feed or care for them again. Too many people think they don't deserve to set limits. That it's mean to take care of themselves before others. It's not. It's what it means to be a responsible adult. No one else can care for you to the degree that you can care for yourself. If you're tired, stay home. If you're stir-crazy, go out. Make small commitments to yourself every single day, and keep them (I will walk for five minutes. I will drink water throughout the day. I will not answer the phone when I'm tapped out).

The Cost of Seeing

Once you understand the frameworks in this book, you will start to see these patterns everywhere. It will be very clear to you when someone is grandstanding for a power play, throwing a two-year-old-style tantrum, or putting other people down to push their pedestal up.

You will be able to see patterns where other people see chaos; you will be able to identify relevant tool kits and step into agency as other people spin out. This level of discernment can save you and the things you care about time and again.

I think discernment is a great gift. But, it also comes at a cost, one that people do not talk about enough. When you see things other people can't see—because they are stuck in repetitive patterns they can't break free of, or because they refuse to engage in reality—it can be lonely.

Because, you can only lead a horse to water—you cannot make it drink. Other people will refuse to see what you show them, until they are ready. Do not try to drag them down the path. Instead, hold the light on the path, so that when they are ready, they can take the first steps themselves.

Ignorance may be bliss. But knowledge is safety.

Parting Words: I Am Water

Sometimes, I think of many people as being like hard, lumpy wooden figures. And I am like a bowl of water. I am transparent; you can see through me. My intentions and motives are clear. I am fluid, I am flexible, I move to fill the shape of my container. I am soothing; I am gentle; I am powerful; I am unstoppable. I shape the world around me.

But, also, I am reflective. I show people a very clear view of themselves, in all their sharp angles. So, many people try to punch me or squash me, wanting to destroy that image—but I slip through their fingers, and they are left feeling wet and foolish.

Most people assume that power comes from hardness—
from being immovable, unyielding, rigid.

But in deep dysfunction,
hardness is fragility.

Hard things can be shattered.
Hard things can be broken.

Water cannot.
You don't win by overpowering them.
You win by being uncapturable—
by reflecting back their failures without absorbing their fear, their trauma, or their violence.

You reveal.
You move.
You endure.

They rage.
They swing.
They exhaust themselves.

And the world around you slowly reshapes itself by your presence, even if they never understand how it happened. Being transparent is dangerous in a world built on lies.

Being reflective is dangerous in a world addicted to self-deception.

Being fluid is dangerous in a world that demands rigid allegiances.

And yet:
It is exactly those qualities that will outlast the collapse of brittle structures.

You will not be the one shattering on the ground when the weight becomes unbearable.

You will be the one who still moves, still reflects, still nourishes new growth when the wreckage clears.

You already are. You are enough, even if after you, all that remains is a ripple, a glint of water in a broken world thirsty for its own reflection.

Be water. And know that if you ever lose sight of yourself, you can always catch a glimpse of yourself, in me.

Acknowledgments

Thank you to Shea, for keeping me healthy so I could write. May DHL, UPS, and FedEx rue the day they met you.

Thank you to my friends, for reflecting my light back to me.

Thank you to Annie and Emmy, for brightening my days. I will always do my best to look after you as well as you look after me.

Thank you to every teacher and classmate at the Remedial People School, for putting me back together.

Thank you to my team at Girl Friday, for understanding my vision and making this book a reality.

Thank you to all of my doctors, coaches, and counselors, who brought me back to life so that I could write this book.

Thank you to Tamora Pierce, for teaching me that anyone can be a hero if they believe in themself, and work both hard and smart.

Thank you to my professors and teachers, who opened my eyes.

Thank you to James Hartley, Robert Putnam, Marcus Aurelius, Annette Lareau, Steven Levitt, John Wooden, Bessel van der Kolk, Pete Walker, Les Carter, Nicole LePera, Lindsay Gibson, Adam Grant, Alice Miller, Janina Fisher, and all of the other sociologists, economists, psychologists, coaches, and leadership experts I have had the privilege to study over the years.

Thank you to those who write the shows, music, and books that make me laugh, help me to see, and make me feel less alone.

Thank you to the team of people (Matt, Liz, Justin, Derek, David, Colby) who manage the complexities of my life with creativity, warmth, and compassion, as I launch myself into new adventures. Thank you for sticking with me, and for saying "Yes, and . . ." when I decided to write a book, a comedy special, a music album, an advocacy project, and a business plan while training a service dog, entering into lawsuits, building AI tools, undergoing medical treatment, and moving around the world. Your ability to be excited, instead of fazed by my enthusiasm will never cease to delight me.

Thank you to anyone who picks up this book, and gives it a chance.

About the Author

Photo © Dimitri Maisuradze

KATE LOWRY is a CEO coach, venture capitalist, and author based in Silicon Valley. Her work focuses on activating agency and helping people be more connected, strategic, and hopeful. She strives to help everyone she interacts with—readers, clients, and friends—to process difficult realities with grace.

An expert in fear-based leaders, Kate developed her methodology growing up in a personal fear-based regime, then refined her approach in the elite worlds of start-ups, private equity, management consulting, and big tech. Her greatest wish is that people facing bullies in the world know that they are not alone, and that they are more powerful than they realize.

Her coaching practice works primarily with mission-driven, underrepresented start-up CEOs, and her writing, both nonfiction and comedy, focuses on equipping people with the skills they need to live their best lives and on helping the world feel warmer and more human.

In Kate's free time, you can find her writing music and comedy specials, exploring the local food scene, and cuddling her service dog, Annie.

www.ingramcontent.com/pod-product-compliance
Lightning Source LLC
Chambersburg PA
CBHW020538030426
42337CB00013B/899